ENSURING

EXCELLENCE

CAMPAIGN

2006—2011

CHAPEL HILL
PUBLIC LIBRARY
FOUNDATION

www.chplfoundation.org

True Stories of
Teens in the Holocaust

COURAGEOUS
TEEN
RESISTERS

PRIMARY
SOURCES
FROM THE
HOLOCAUST

Other Titles in the
True Stories of
Teens in the Holocaust
Series

ESCAPE—TEENS ON THE RUN
PRIMARY SOURCES FROM THE HOLOCAUST
ISBN-13: 978-0-7660-3270-5

HIDDEN TEENS,
HIDDEN LIVES
PRIMARY SOURCES FROM THE HOLOCAUST
ISBN-13: 978-0-7660-3271-2

SHATTERED YOUTH
IN NAZI GERMANY
PRIMARY SOURCES FROM THE HOLOCAUST
ISBN-13: 978-0-7660-3268-2

TRAPPED—YOUTH IN THE
NAZI GHETTOS
PRIMARY SOURCES FROM THE HOLOCAUST
ISBN-13: 978-0-7660-3272-9

YOUTH DESTROYED—THE NAZI CAMPS
PRIMARY SOURCES FROM THE HOLOCAUST
ISBN-13: 978-0-7660-3273-6

CONTENTS

Acknowledgments

Special thanks to the United States Holocaust Memorial Museum in Washington, D.C., and the USC Shoah Foundation Institute for all their help in completing this book.

Introduction

The day had finally come. After months of planning, everything was in place. This day had been put off too many times, but now it was finally here. Samuel Willenberg could feel it the moment he awoke: "We arose from our bunks, excited and tense. . . . Our hearts were overflowing with hatred and with the desire for revenge."[1]

Willenberg had reason to hate. He was a prisoner in Treblinka, a Nazi death camp. All the Jews in his town of Opatów, Poland, had been brought there to die. He was only nineteen, yet he had already seen hundreds killed before his eyes.

Treblinka was two camps: a work camp and a death camp. Willenberg had lied, telling the Nazis that he was a brick mason. The lie, together with his youth and strength, had allowed him into the work camp. On this day, he was going to get out.

About a hundred men in Treblinka had plotted to set both camps on fire and break free. They had gotten access to weapons. Willenberg described the plan:

> We were divided into groups, each of which
> was assigned a specific task. Some had
> instructions to kill the sentries in the
> watchtowers, others to storm the barracks
> with hand grenades, and still others to
> fall upon the SS men [Nazi guards] who
> walked about in the camp. . . . We had

```
planned to cut the telephone lines, to set
afire the gasoline dump.²
```

For such bold resistance, timing was important. The revolt would take place in the afternoon, when the guards were tired. The men would have just enough daylight to carry out the attack and then the cover of darkness under which to escape. The time was set for 4:30 P.M. Everyone would have to do his part at precisely the same moment—they had to take the Nazi guards by surprise. The signal to act would be a single rifle shot. Willenberg was eager to act:

```
Two prisoners . . . locked themselves in
the arsenal and began to pass out rifles,
ammunition and hand grenades . . . to the
construction workers, who were in on the
conspiracy. . . . The grenades were taken
in buckets covered with rags. Everything
was placed beneath piles of potatoes.³
```

At four o'clock, everything was going according to plan. But then something went dreadfully wrong. A prisoner was found with a coin, a crime the Nazis deemed deserving of death. At Treblinka, punishment was swift and sure. A guard dragged the man to the place of execution and killed him with a single rifle shot.

The sound stunned the conspirators. It was too early. Many firearms still lay under potatoes in the center of the camp. Without them, people could not carry out their assigned tasks. Willenberg, like many others, had not yet received his weapons. Should he hurry to the buckets of grenades or make a run for the fence to escape? The scene was a nightmare of confusion and panic: "Shots rained down. . . . The roar of an explosion shook the air. . . .

Prisoners came running from everywhere. . . . Now the barracks are on fire. . . . The machine gun from the nearby watchtower spews forth burst after burst of fire."[4]

Willenberg grabbed a gun from a comrade who was petrified with fear. He squeezed the trigger three times; a guard dropped and a machine gun fell silent. Behind him the camp was in flames. In front, beyond a sea of dead prisoners, were the barbed-wire fence and antitank barriers. He dropped to his knees. Two years later, he remembered the moment vividly:

> "I ascend the bridge of corpses. I hear a shot, feel a blow, but one more jump and I am at the edge of the woods."

```
I crawl along in the
exposed area and reach the barriers. . . .
The machine gun is still firing away, but
we can no longer remain here. With one leap
I ascend the bridge of corpses. I hear a
shot, feel a blow, but one more jump and I
am at the edge of the woods.⁵
```

Willenberg was one of the fortunate ones. Eight hundred men tried to escape that day, August 2, 1943. Half never made it beyond the fence. Of those who did, about three hundred were hunted down by the camp guards and shot. Only forty were alive at the end of the war.[6] Forty out of eight hundred—that is only 5 percent.

Those who died at Treblinka were victims of what historians call the Holocaust. The Nazi Party of Germany, led by Adolf Hitler, tried to rid Europe of all its Jews. From 1933 to 1945, the party murdered 11 million people. Six million were Jews.

Of these, 1.5 million were children. The Nazis shot them in the streets, starved them in gated ghettos, and executed them in death camps like Treblinka.

How could this happen to so many people? Did they not fight back? Was there no resistance to such brutality? Yes, there was resistance. Brave people—men, women, and children—stood up to the evil. But might was on the side of their oppressors. For people like Willenberg who resisted the Nazi brutality, the odds of survival were always stacked heavily against them.

Chapter One

LIVING WITH PERSECUTION

Jews had lived with discrimination for generations. Antisemitism—prejudice against Jewish people—was especially strong in the early 1900s in France, Germany, Poland, Russia, and much of Eastern Europe. Non-Jews looked at Jews as inferior. They did not try to hide their prejudice. A Jewish man from Poland described how open the antisemitism was at that time in his country:

> We knew that they hated us, because in Poland, there was nothing hidden. Ever since I could remember as a child going to school, I would see on the street—be it on a fence or on a building of a Jewish home or in front on a Jewish store or on the sidewalk—there were signs, we call it graffiti here today, signs all over the place: "Jew Go to Palestine. You Filthy Jew, We Don't Want You in Poland."[1]

Even small children accepted separation and discrimination as facts of life. They learned that Jewish boys and girls did not play with Gentile (non-Jewish) children. Mary Antin, a Jewish girl in Russia, explained that such knowledge was simply a part of being Jewish:

> I do not know when I became old enough to understand. . . . There was no time in my

Mary Antin (left) and her sister Fetchke. Mary Antin learned to deal with antisemitism at a young age in Russia.

life when I did not hear and see and feel the truth. . . . But for a long while I did not understand. Then there came a time when I knew that . . . the world was divided into Jews and Gentiles. This knowledge came so gradually that it could not shock me. It trickled into my consciousness drop by drop.[2]

In some places, Jews shielded themselves from the worst of the abuse. They lived in Jewish neighborhoods and kept to themselves. But the two worlds sometimes intersected. When they did, antisemitism nearly always presented itself. Mary Antin described how living with abuse became a routine:

The first time Vanka threw mud at me, I ran home and complained to my mother, who brushed off my dress and said, quite resignedly, "How can I help you, my poor child? Vanka is a Gentile. The Gentiles do as they like with us Jews." The next time Vanka abused me, I did not cry, but ran for

> shelter, saying to myself, "Vanka is a
> Gentile." The third time, when Vanka spat
> on me, I wiped my face and thought nothing
> at all. I accepted ill-usage from the
> Gentiles as one accepts the weather. The
> world was made in a certain way, and I had
> to live in it.[3]

Before 1933, Jewish and non-Jewish children in Germany usually got along, despite the antisemitism. Henry Landman recalled that religion had little importance in school:

> I played hard with both my Jewish friends
> and my Gentile friends from school. There
> were only two of us who were Jews in my
> class, so that most of my friends there
> were Gentiles. We never made an issue about
> it. We were just classmates and I went
> to all their parties. . . . We learned,
> played, studied, and got into mischief
> together. No mention was made about where
> we prayed, or how. What counted then was
> how fast, or smart you were. Period. I
> had lots of Jewish friends too; but, again,
> they were first friends and, secondly,
> Jewish.[4]

Antisemitism Intensifies

After Hitler became chancellor (leader) of Germany in 1933, however, things were different. It was as though the prejudice against Jews that boiled just below the surface of everyday life burst through everywhere. By that time, Landman was in Gymnasium, or high school. He wrote of the change:

It was during my later Gymnasium days that I first encountered open anti-Semitism. The hatred for the Jewish student started first in the Gymnasium. It had only now begun to trickle down to the younger children. The boys from other schools, or even my own, would taunt me on the way to and from school. I could hear the words, "Sau Jud," or "Jewish Pig"! I couldn't understand this. I would go home and ask my parents why the other children would call me such terrible names; I didn't even know some of them.[5]

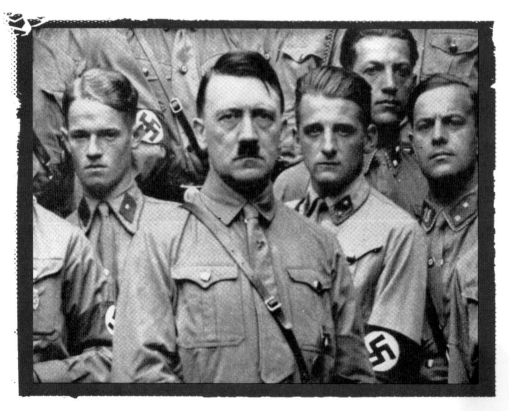

Adolf Hitler became chancellor of Germany in 1933. This photo of him was taken shortly after his appointment.

Even very young children noticed the difference after Hitler came to power. Carola Stern Steinhardt was only eight, but she felt the suddenly harsher tone:

> I had lots of German friends. . . . But it changed, it changed in 1933. It changed a lot. . . . I had one girl which really was my idol. . . . We played together, and at one point she said to me, "You know, Carola, I can't play with you anymore."
>
>   And I said, "How come?"
>
>   She said, "Because you're a Jew."
>
>   I said, "What is that?"
>
>   She said, "Well, have you heard of Hitler?"
>
>   I said yes. "Yes, because every morning they used to say 'Heil Hitler.' But why can't you play with me anymore? Why?"
>
>   She said, "Because my father told me that you're Jewish, and Gentile children, Aryan kids, can no longer play with the Jewish kids." . . . And that was very, very hard for an eight-year-old.[6]

The abuse of children did not come just from their classmates. Teachers also singled out their Jewish students. In the 1930s, this happened mostly in Germany. Lore Metzger described how she felt when the change came to her school:

> In school, Jewish students, who were now referred to as non-Arians [sic], were segregated from their fellow Arian [sic] students and were assigned to sit in a special corner of the classroom. During the recreation period we [had] to use a special

place in the school yard in order not to get into physical contact with our fellow-students.

To have to sit in the so-called Jew corner, to have to listen to the most degrading remarks and to have to avoid all contact with my classmates, who until now had been my friends, made these school years a period of torment and agony for me.[7]

The prejudice and mistreatment spilled beyond the classroom to the athletic field. Gad Beck remembered being allowed to compete in a race but not to receive his prize:

Antisemitism spilled out of the classroom and affected children in many aspects of life. Gad Beck (above) competed in track and field but was not allowed to receive his prize.

I was selected to run in a 4 x 60 meter relay at the Youths sports festival in Weissensee. . . . I run last and win. Yep, ha, that was the highlight. . . . I went back to the teacher. "No," he said, "Of course you can't go on the podium, man. You are not allowed to return the German Salute." And he put another boy on the

podium. I can still see it. I was leaning
against a poplar tree . . . and cried
horribly.[8]

Outside the school, in city sports and public places, Jews were excluded. The pain and humiliation haunted Guy Stern into his adult years:

There was a young man whom we knew from the
swimming pool and when it was still open to
Jews we would go swimming there, my brother
and I, and one time a young fellow about
our age started beating us up and if we
had really resisted that would have made it
worse. . . . There were many places where
you couldn't go on vacation any more. These
were mild things, but being beaten up at
the swimming pool, I felt it was getting
worse and worse. . . .

We were on soccer teams together and then
all of a sudden you were not. I was kicked
out of an athletic club. I was [a] fairly
decent athlete and I had won the requisite
number of points to get some sort of medal
and that of course was denied.[9]

Parents felt powerless to fight this terrible humiliation of their children. They responded in the same way their parents and grand-parents dealt with discrimination and abuse. They retreated into their own communities. Fathers and mothers took their children out of the offending schools and put them in Jewish institutions. That is what happened to Carola Stern Steinhardt:

It was very frightening, and, especially
for an eight-year-old child. . . . It

got worse and worse, and by the age of eleven, my parents decided that they couldn't leave me in school anymore. Neither myself nor my sister, and they would send me to a Jewish school. In the meantime they had made Jewish schools all over Germany where only Jewish kids went . . . where some of the children came by bus and some of them stayed in the dorm. And I was sent into the dorm. I was very homesick.[10]

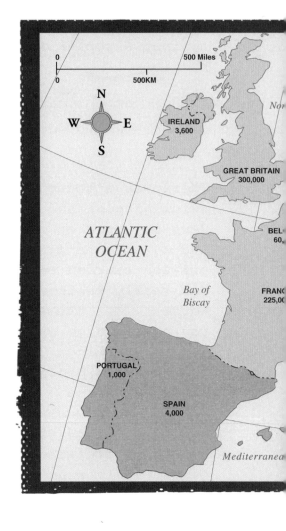

Homesickness and schoolyard taunting were minor problems compared with what was to come. The persecution of Jews reached far beyond the schools, past the children. Jewish men and women were denied jobs, refused medical treatment, and not allowed in many stores. As bad as the discrimination was, many German Jews still assumed it would not last. Their ancestors had suffered through mistreatment and had survived. How bad could

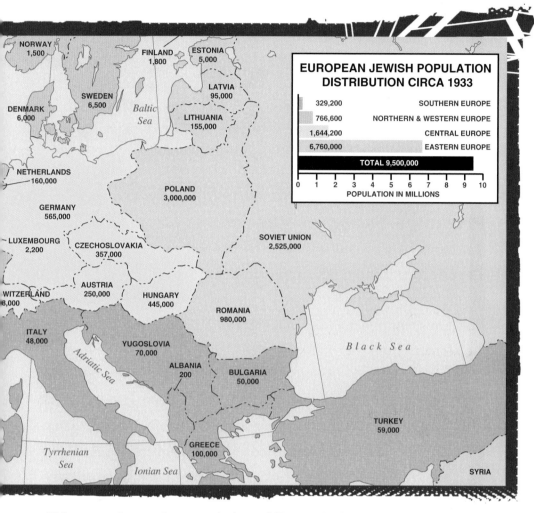

EUROPEAN JEWISH POPULATION DISTRIBUTION CIRCA 1933

Population	Region
329,200	SOUTHERN EUROPE
766,600	NORTHERN & WESTERN EUROPE
1,644,200	CENTRAL EUROPE
6,760,000	EASTERN EUROPE
TOTAL 9,500,000	

POPULATION IN MILLIONS

0 1 2 3 4 5 6 7 8 9 10

NORWAY 1,500
FINLAND 1,800
ESTONIA 5,000
LATVIA 95,000
SWEDEN 6,500
Baltic Sea
DENMARK 6,000
LITHUANIA 155,000
NETHERLANDS 160,000
POLAND 3,000,000
GERMANY 565,000
LUXEMBOURG 2,200
CZECHOSLOVAKIA 357,000
SOVIET UNION 2,525,000
AUSTRIA 250,000
WITZERLAND 8,000
HUNGARY 445,000
ROMANIA 980,000
ITALY 48,000
YUGOSLOVIA 70,000
Black Sea
ALBANIA 200
BULGARIA 50,000
Adriatic Sea
TURKEY 59,000
Tyrrhenian Sea
GREECE 100,000
Ionian Sea
SYRIA

This map shows the population of Europe's Jews by country around 1933. After Hitler came to power, life for Jews in Europe would never be the same. The Holocaust would change these population figures forever.

things get? Surely they could wait out the storm. That is what Ruth Drescher's father thought:

> [His] attitude had been: "Leave Germany? How could I do that? This is my home. I fought in the war (that would have been the First World War), why, I was even awarded

the Iron Cross. We will be safe here. This Hitler business will pass." And he was by no means unique. I have since spoken to many people who recall their fathers in precisely the same way. Yes, they were Jews, but they were Germans first and found it inconceivable that they could be treated in anything less than a respectful way.[11]

Prejudice Becomes Violent

But they *were* treated with disrespect—unbelievable disrespect. The mistreatment did not simply grow worse gradually. It erupted in one twenty-four-hour period in a frenzy of fire and violence. Ruth Drescher remembered that night as the event "which removed the blinders from [her father's] eyes."[12]

On the evening of November 9, 1938, in cities all over Germany and Austria, gangs of Nazi storm troopers descended on Jewish homes and businesses. They carried axes, hammers, clubs, and bricks. While the police stood silently by, the men smashed the windows of thousands of Jewish stores. They set

> They set more than one thousand synagogues on fire.

more than one thousand synagogues on fire. They dragged Jews from their homes and beat them, killing ninety-one. They arrested more than thirty thousand Jewish men between sixteen and sixty years of age and took them to concentration camps.[13]

That night became known as *Kristallnacht*, the Night of Broken Glass. The Nazis claimed it was a spontaneous reaction to a crime committed by a seventeen-year-old Jew. The young man, Herschel Grynszpan, very angry over the harsh treatment of his family, had assassinated a German official. But the rampage was carefully coordinated, charging through cities and villages from one end of the country to another at exactly the same moment. It marked the beginning of the undisguised war against Europe's Jews.

All night long and the entire next day the devastation and looting continued. How could anyone fight against it? It came suddenly, without warning. Government officials and ordinary citizens carried out the attacks. It was senseless and out of control. Who could resist? Miriam Litke was only a little girl, but she knew there was no way to stop it:

> When the Jewish shops were being broken into, the plate-glass display windows shattered, looting and destroying of goods continuing, my relatives who lived nearby called me. My Uncle . . . owned a large furniture store on the Kastonienallee, a beautiful boulevard lined with chestnut trees. He asked me to go there and watch what was happening to his store and to see that the "employees don't steal"! Thinking back one can see how ludicrous was the idea to send an eleven-year-old child to watch the Nazi destruction of his store. But my uncle with his beard certainly could not go there, neither could his grown sons, so they sent me, a fair-skinned, light-haired, blue-eyed girl with pigtails. I stood there with a crowd of people who were obviously enjoying the "show." What was I supposed to do? Keep anyone from looting?[14]

The only possible form of resistance was hiding men from the massive arrests. In this way, children helped. Walter Kopfstein, a religious Jew, suspected his name was on the list of Berlin citizens marked for the concentration camps. So he devised a code with his family. If his wife or child uttered the words "There are guests," he would know that the Nazis were looking for him. On the morning of Kristallnacht, he made his way past the shards of glass to his office. His wife and thirteen-year-old son, Max, stayed home, afraid to step out of their apartment. Max described what happened when the doorbell rang:

> There stood two Gestapo agents in civilian clothes, asking to see my father, Walter Kopfstein. She [his mother] answered that he was in his office, at the same time giving me a sign with her hand behind her back. I went downstairs via the back entrance to our flat, and ran to the public phone booth at the corner of the street, where I phoned my father in his office to say "There are guests."[15]

Max's father escaped that day, but that day marked only the beginning.

Chapter Two

REBEL GROUPS IN GERMANY

Not all Gentile Germans held prejudices against Jews. Not everyone threw bricks or cheered on the Night of Broken Glass. Some wept as they watched the vicious attack. Others were angered by its harshness. A few decided to resist the Nazi brutality.

Walter Meyer decided to do something. He was twelve years old on Kristallnacht, and he never forgot the fiery scene. He knew then that he, like his father, did not like Nazis. But a year and a half later, Hitler had started what became World War II and Meyer joined the Hitler Youth.

He had little choice. Every Aryan boy in Germany between the ages of fourteen and eighteen was required to be part of the youth organization.[1] Children who did not join could be taken from their parents and placed in orphanages. So Meyer's father reluctantly permitted him to enroll.

At first, the Hitler Youth was a little like the Boy Scouts. But, gradually, the groups began to look like junior armies. The boys wore military-type uniforms. They learned to march and handle weapons. Meyer decided to resist being part of Hitler's antisemitic regime. He dropped out of the Hitler Youth and organized a small group of boys who felt the same way he did—angry:

> We resented those punks who wanted to tell
> us what to do and what not to do and we

were supposed to salute them. . . . We all got together and said, "Did you see [that Hitler Youth]? You see he's got a star now? We're supposed to salute him. Let's make life difficult for him."[2]

Edelweiss Pirates

Meyer's group was one of several in the large cities of Germany. They were small, usually ten or fifteen members. They called themselves "pirates." They wore badges or pins that depicted an edelweiss, a small flower. Eventually all of the groups became known as the Edelweiss Pirates. As the anti-Hitler Youth, they made fun of the Nazis. For the most part, they were not concerned with the bigger picture of what was happening in Germany. They were simply working class, non-Jewish children who did not like what they saw around them. When asked about the purpose of the Edelweiss Pirates, Meyer explained:

Walter Meyer was a member of the Edelweiss Pirates. His anti-Nazi activities would get him into serious trouble.

If . . . forced to give you one word I would say anti-authority . . . coupled with lust for adventure. . . .

> It's like a gang. I resented authority. . . .
> I was much too young to understand [about
> Hitler and what was going on with the
> Jews]. . . . Some of the older ones
> actually had ideological ideas. This is
> probably why some of the guys who met with
> me were later kind of glorified. . . . But
> why do you [join] a gang? Because you're
> bored, because you don't like what goes on,
> in terms of some weirdos becoming lieuten-
> ants and captains and so on, and you want
> to have a little fun. You get the attention
> that you don't get at home. That combina-
> tion makes you do certain things.[3]

The "certain things" the pirates did grew into small acts of resistance against the Nazis. At first, their activities seemed harmless:

> We had meetings. . . . We would ask . . .
> what are we going to do next and maybe one
> would say . . . the Hitler Youths, they all
> stored their equipment at such and such a
> place, let's make it disappear. Okay, when
> are we going to meet, such and such a time,
> and that's what we did. It . . . came to
> the point where we became enemies and peo-
> ple began to look for us because we went a
> little too drastic, you know we started by
> deflating the tires, then we made the whole
> bicycle disappear, so it came to the point
> where too many complained.[4]

As the war continued, the pirates became more daring. Much of their early activity amounted to little more than youthful pranks. They painted anti-Hitler slogans on walls. They hurled bricks through the windows of war factories. They poured sugar water into the gas tanks of soldiers' cars. But their small acts of defiance grew larger. They stole explosives and gave them to adult resistance groups. They derailed army supply trains. They hid army deserters and escaped prisoners.[5]

Such rebellious acts may seem small, but punishment for those acts was usually harsh. Arrests and beatings were the least of the possibilities. Some who were caught were taken to concentration camps. Some were tortured. Others were shot or hanged. Despite the consequences, Meyer and the other pirates persisted in their resistance of the Nazis.

"Do you realize the penalty for looting is death?"

Dusseldorf, Meyer's home city, had a prison camp for French soldiers captured in the war. Because Meyer spoke French, he served as a runner, taking food and information to the prisoners. Those acts of mercy cost him dearly. During an air raid in early 1943, he was near the camp:

> We knew by the shaking that a bomb had dropped rather close by, so we went out. . . . We found a shoe store, totally destroyed and the shoes were everywhere. So I said, "Come on, let's pick up shoes." Put the shoes in my coat; it was winter. Then we walked towards the main square where there were a few lights where the bunker was, and . . . a lady [from the prisoner of war camp] came out. . . . And I said, "Do you want these shoes?"
>
> There was a policeman close by [who] said, "What's going on here?" And as he

approached us I started running. And he
screamed, "Hold him! Hold him!" for maybe
six, seven, eight blocks down the street.
Somebody opened his arms like a bear and
held me and from there I went to the police
station. And the one who tried to arrest
me showed up and whipped me very nicely,
making clear that you shouldn't escape from
a German police officer.[6]

Meyer was sixteen at the time. The police interrogated him at
the police station:

I was in the main police headquarters. I
had already been caned for fleeing the
scene earlier. The banging from the hallway
becoming louder. An SS officer was coming
to fetch me and the sound of his boots was
ricocheting down the corridor and into the
little room where I was waiting. It was an
impressive sound. . . .
    "Why did you take the shoes?"
    "I don't know."
    "Do you realize the penalty for looting
is death?"
    From there I spent maybe two hours.
Questions and questions. . . . The first
man sat in front of me and stared coldly
into my eyes, while the second relentlessly
beckoned forward across the back of the
room. "And where were you before the air
raid?" he asked. The tone in his voice
suggested that he already knew the answer.
    "Some friends, we were socializing."
    "Liar!" he shouted. "You were with a
group of boys planning subversive activities

against the Hitler Youth. We know about
your involvement in the Edelweiss Pirates,
and we know you sympathize with the
French."[7]

The charges were true and he had been caught. His young age
did not matter:

From there . . . I was transferred to
Gestapo [Nazi police] headquarters. . . .
I was beaten, kicked and I had to clean my
own blood and my own vomit. . . . Then I
was transferred from there, early in the
morning to [another] prison. . . . I was in
a cell, concrete floor and it was very much
like taking an African lion and put him in
a cage. I was a wild boy. I didn't belong
into a cage.[8]

Meyer remained in that cell for a few months. Then he finally
went to trial:

My trial, the state attorney . . . asked
for the death penalty. The judge and the
state attorney and somebody else, some
functionary, they kind of argued about
whether it was looting, or whether it
was theft. The idea was that the two had
different consequences. And so they retired
and when we came back, the judge decided
. . . this man [Meyer], having had intimate
contact with our enemy, and being the
leader of the Edelweiss [Pirates], having
destroyed state goods, and state property,
does not deserve any kind of consideration.
So when the judge came back and said, on
the grounds of his outstanding involvement

Hitler Youth members sit in a stadium. When Meyer was arrested and questioned, he was accused of "planning subversive activities against the Hitler Youth." The Edelweiss Pirates rebelled against Nazi-controlled organizations like the Hitler Youth.

> in athleticism, and considering age and circumstances, I condemn you to one to four years in prison.[9]

After the trial, Meyer went to prison. He remained, in his words, "a wild boy," trying unsuccessfully to escape. He was offered a deal: Join the German army or be sent to a concentration camp. He chose the camp and spent the next year in Ravensbruck. Despite the harsh conditions there, the "wild boy" managed to escape.

For many years after World War II, most Germans thought of the Edelweiss Pirates as gangs of wild, lawless boys. But in 1988, Yad Vashem, the Holocaust Memorial in Jerusalem, recognized the Edelweiss Pirates as "Righteous Among the Nations." It is a designation given to people and groups that demonstrated extraordinary bravery, at the risk of their own lives, to help Jews during the Holocaust. More than forty years after their small but courageous deeds, these groups were officially recognized as heroes and resistance fighters.

Herbert Baum Group

While they were still able, some young people in Germany resisted the Nazi government. Many of the resisters were Communists. They admired what they saw in the Soviet Union: the common people overthrowing an aristocratic government. Communists in Germany wanted the people to rebel against the leaders of their country. In the 1920s, a number of young Jews joined the Communist movement.

Herbert Baum joined the movement at the age of fourteen. When Hitler came to power, Baum was twenty-one. With his wife and others, Baum formed what became known as the Baum Group in Berlin. Ellen Arndt described the little band: "They were . . . young people, most of them Jewish. They were Communists. Their aim was to interrupt [sabotage] whatever they could in Germany."[10]

At first, the group operated openly. Members handed out leaflets that warned people of the dangers of Nazism. They published a newspaper. Eventually, speaking out against the government became too dangerous, so the group went underground—that is, they went about their activities in secret. They broke into several smaller groups so that if one group ran into trouble, the others could still function. Arndt explained how they operated:

These people were very careful. You only dealt with one. He would simply say to me, "Can you give me a hand? I'm making something that's needed." And of course I would. Course at night not all machines are running. He would fashion things on the machines for bombs, explosives. And then you had to get it out of the plant. And we had a guard who would check us when we went out. The guard, very fortunately, was an old guy and . . . we would pell mell rush by him and he wouldn't see or hear much. And then he did check your—made you open your purse. Of course you had nothing in it. I remember taking the detonator out in the bra. He wasn't to check that, right?[11]

"He would simply say to me, 'Can you give me a hand? I'm making something that's needed.'"

Arndt, who was eighteen at that time, described how the group managed to get the materials for its sabotage activities:

They needed cable to detonate the bombs so we would take another guy and say, "Go into this room and undress to your shorts." [W]e would bind cable from his underarms to his hips and put the clothes back on and he'd get the cable out. And so by and by stuff got out and it was really—in hindsight, we really shouldn't have done it because it cost a lot of lives.[12]

How many lives did such activities cost? More than were affiliated with the Baum Group. The group performed few acts of sabotage before its last, most dramatic, and costliest act. In May 1942, with the German army advancing deep into the Soviet Union, the Nazis set up an exhibit in Berlin that condemned the Communist Soviet Union as well as Jews. This angered the Communist Jews of the Baum Group. They decided to take major action:

> They set a bomb off at an exhibit that was called the Soviet exhibit. It was against Russia. It would have been better had we bombed the train. No! An exhibit. This group blew up the exhibit in protest, so to speak. And of course, everybody got caught and everybody got executed. . . . Everybody got guillotined.[13]

Twenty-two people were executed for their part in the bombing. Others were placed in prison and eventually killed at the Auschwitz death camp. Herbert Baum was tortured, and he died while still in prison. The Nazis punished any resistance against them, and their punishment was always harsher than the offense itself. No one was hurt in the explosion at the exhibit, but the Gestapo, the Nazi police, arrested five hundred Jews and had them shot. They were to serve as examples of what happens to people who defied Nazi rule.

The White Rose

By the time of the Baum Group's executions, very few Jews still lived in Germany. Within months of Kristallnacht, nearly half of Germany's five hundred thousand Jews had fled to other countries in Europe and elsewhere. Over the next three years, thousands more were deported. By 1943, only about fifteen thousand Jews remained.[14] For them, resistance meant almost certain death. But non-Jews continued to resist the Nazi government as well. Many of the Gentile resisters were young people.

Hans and Sophie Scholl were college students. They were loyal German citizens and leaders in the Hitler Youth. Hans had carried the Nazi flag at a rally and served in the German army. But the brother and sister watched in horror as the Nazi government rounded up Jews and forced them to work at degrading jobs. Then, in church, they listened in stunned silence as their bishop described more of the cruelties of the Hitler regime. He explained that the Nazi government was killing children and adults they considered mentally deficient. The Scholls decided they needed to get this information to others.

They found others on their campus, the University of Munich, who shared their disgust toward Nazi policies. Fellow students Christoph Probst, Alexander Schmorell, and Willi Graf and Professor Kurt Huber joined them. The six formed what they called the White Rose resistance group. In their first act of defiance, they made copies of the bishop's sermon. They printed it in a leaflet they called "The White Rose."

At the university, they posted the leaflets anywhere they thought someone might find and read them. The papers criticized the government's actions and called on German citizens to refuse to go along with those actions: "Every individual, conscious of his responsibility as a member of Christian and Western civilization, must defend himself against the scourges of mankind, against fascism [Nazism] and any similar system of totalitarianism.

Pictured in front of Sophie Scholl, from left to right: Hurbert Furtwaengler, Hans Scholl, Sawmiller (first name unknown), and Alexander Schmorell. The Scholl siblings and Schmorell were members of the White Rose.

Offer passive resistance—*resistance*—wherever you may be . . . before it is too late."[15]

The White Rose resistance group illustrated the depths to which the government had sunk by pointing out what it had done to its Jewish citizens. In its second leaflet, Hans and Sophie Scholl argued:

> Since the conquest of Poland three hundred thousand Jews have been murdered in this country [Germany] in the most bestial way. Here we see the most frightful crime against human dignity, a crime that is unparalleled in the whole of history. For Jews, too, are human beings—no matter what position we take with respect to the Jewish question—and a crime of this dimension has been perpetrated against human beings.[16]

By the time the White Rose leaflets appeared, the murderous Nazi schemes were becoming evident. Their second leaflet admonished its readers: "You are fully aware of [the atrocities]— or if not of these, then of other equally grave crimes committed

Christoph Probst was one of five students at the University of Munich to help form the White Rose. Probst shared the Scholl siblings' disgust toward Nazi policies.

by this frightful sub-humanity."[17] It called upon all Germans to rise up and overthrow the leaders who perpetrated such evil:

> It is not too late, however, to do away with this most reprehensible of all miscarriages of government. . . . Now, when in recent years our eyes have been opened, when we know exactly who our adversary is, it is high time to root out this brown horde. Up until the outbreak of the war the larger part of the German people were blinded; the Nazis did not show themselves in their true aspect. But now, now that we have recognized them for what they are, it

Alexander Schmorell was a member of the White Rose.

EIN DEUTSCHES FLUGBLATT

DIES ist der Text eines deutschen Flugblatts, von dem ein Exemplar nach England gelangt ist. Studenten der Universität München haben es im Februar dieses Jahres verfasst und in der Universität verteilt. Sechs von ihnen sind dafür hingerichtet worden, andere wurden eingesperrt, andere strafweise an die Front geschickt. Seither werden auch an allen anderen deutschen Universitäten die Studenten ,,ausgesiebt''. Das Flugblatt drückt also offenbar die Gesinnungen eines beträchtlichen Teils der deutschen Studenten aus.

Aber es sind nicht nur die Studenten. In allen Schichten gibt es Deutsche, die Deutschlands wirkliche Lage erkannt haben ; Goebbels schimpft sie ,,die Objektiven''. Ob Deutschland noch selber sein Schicksal wenden kann, hängt davon ab, dass diese Menschen sich zusammenfinden und handeln. Das weiss Goebbels, und deswegen beteuert er krampfhaft, ,,dass diese Sorte Mensch zahlenmässig nicht ins Gewicht fällt''. Sie sollen nicht wissen, wie viele sie sind.

Wir werden den Krieg sowieso gewinnen. Aber wir sehen nicht ein, warum die Vernünftigen und Anständigen in Deutschland nicht zu Worte kommen sollen. Deswegen werfen die Flieger der RAF zugleich mit ihren Bomben jetzt dieses Flugblatt, für das sechs junge Deutsche gestorben sind, und das die Gestapo natürlich sofort konfisziert hat, in Millionen von Exemplaren über Deutschland ab.

Manifest der Münchner Studenten

Erschüttert steht unser Volk vor dem Untergang der Männer von Stalingrad, 330.000 deutsche Männer hat die geniale Strategie des Weltkriegsgefreiten sinn- und verantwortungslos in Tod und Verderben gehetzt. Führer, wir danken Dir !

Es gärt im deutschen Volk. Wollen wir weiter einem Dilettanten das Schicksal unserer Armeen anvertrauen ? Wollen wir den niedrigsten Machtinstinkten einer Parteiclique den Rest der deutschen Jugend opfern ? Nimmermehr !

Der Tag der Abrechnung ist gekommen, der Abrechnung unserer deutschen Jugend mit der verabscheuungswürdigsten Tyrannei, die unser Volk je erduldet hat. Im Namen des ganzen deutschen Volkes fordern wir von dem Staat Adolf Hitlers die persönliche Freiheit, das kostbarste Gut der Deutschen zurück, um das er uns in der erbärmlichsten Weise betrogen hat.

In einem Staat rücksichtsloser Knebelung jeder freien Meinungsäußerung sind wir aufgewachsen.

This is a page from the final anti-Nazi leaflet written and distributed by the White Rose resistance group in February 1943.

must be the sole and first duty, the holiest duty of every German to destroy these beasts.[18]

During 1942 and 1943, the group printed six leaflets. Merely possessing—much less printing and distributing—such anti-Nazi pamphlets was illegal. Still they persisted. The group expanded into an organization of students in other German cities. They mailed the leaflets to other colleges. The leaflets—the "leaves of the White Rose"—could be found all over Germany and Austria. Members of the society also painted their beliefs and hopes on walls throughout Munich: "Down with Hitler" . . . "Hitler the Mass Murderer" . . . and "Freedom."

But on February 18, 1943, their resistance ended abruptly. Hans and Sophie went to school before classes started. They placed their pamphlets in hallways and classrooms. Then, Hans and Sophie climbed the stairs to the top floor and Sophie dropped the last of the leaflets into the atrium below. The head janitor spotted her and she was arrested. Four days later, the two Scholls and Christoph Probst were tried and convicted of treason. The next day they walked calmly, with their heads held high, to the guillotine. The other three members of the White Rose, Schmorell, Graf, and Professor Huber, were captured shortly afterward and also beheaded. Hans's last words were the cry of the resistance: "Long live freedom!"

For most of the Jews of Europe, however, freedom would never come.

Chapter Three

RESISTANCE IN WESTERN EUROPE

After 1940, most of Western Europe was not free. Hitler's armies had roared across the continent, swallowing one nation after another. In the conquered countries, movements sprang up that resisted German occupation and oppression. They resisted by sabotaging German interests and sheltering Jews.

In addition to the Jews who lived in the countries of Western Europe before the military invasion, many German Jews had fled to these places. They hoped the Nazi terror would be confined to Germany. As Hitler took over other nations, however, the Nazis hunted down Jews there and imprisoned them in camps. In France, Gaby Cohen, a Jewish girl who had just completed high school, was vaguely aware of the Nazi activity:

> [From 1940] until late 1942 [we heard] many rumors that foreign Jews were being arrested and put into internment camps. Some of the stories were quite horrible: people beaten, tortured, sent off to Eastern Europe. All kinds of things were told, but . . . nobody knew exactly what was happening.[1]

Rescue of Children

Young Cohen decided to find out what was happening and do what she could to help. She went to the office of Oeuvre de Secours aux Enfants (OSE, Work to Rescue the Children) and

By the end of 1940, Germany occupied most of Western Europe. This map shows all the territory Germany occupied at the end of 1940.

volunteered to work in the camps. She found that this organization, together with the Eclaireurs Israelites de France (EIF, Jewish Scouts of France) were rescuing children from the Nazi camps, placing some in scout camps, and hiding others in French homes. She found that the resistance was large:

> So many people were part of the effort: Catholic, Protestant, Communist, Left, Right, Jewish, and non-Jewish organizations and individuals. It was really a unique gathering of efforts on behalf of children. American organizations like the Unitarians, the Quakers, and the YWCA fought and fought until they gained authorization to take these children . . . out of the camps.[2]

Margot Blank was in a group that had permission to leave the camp. A refugee from Germany, she was fifteen when France fell to Hitler. The OSE plucked her and about twenty other children from an internment camp and took them to an IEF children's home. Even though the organizations had official approval for their actions at first, the Nazis could change their minds at any time. The rescue agencies and the children had to be secretive. Blank recalled moving from home to home:

> We lived on a farm. We lived in tents. We did our cooking. . . . When it was raining we slept in a barn on that farm. And while we were sleeping one night in that barn, one of the cheftaines [scout leaders] from another children's home also from EIF came in the middle of the night—two o'clock in the morning—and spoke to the cheftaine. . . . They were told that we have to disappear

41

Members of a French Jewish resistance group dance a horah
(a Jewish dance) in their training camp in the Alps in 1943.
Members of this group helped sabotage German army operations
and assisted Jews and prisoners of war escape into safe territory.

because we could be re-deported [sent back to the camp]. So within a few minutes, they woke us all up and took us into the woods. We were huddled together into a little hut when . . . the rain came. Luckily, there were French scouts camping nearby . . . and they were bringing us food. After three days we [were] just told to pack up and to go. And with our knapsacks and a Red Cross box which we changed off carrying . . . we came to a farm and we'd stay and work in the fields for a little bit of food, then we'll go to another farm. . . .

We were told to take our shoes off at night walking through the towns so nobody [would] hear us. We walked to the station and we're in the train and we started to be placed into convents. We also had one condition—that if any one of us is recognized by anyone—not to tell we are part of a group but that we just happened to meet so we would not involve anybody else.[3]

The care these rescue groups took paid off. During the German occupation, eleven thousand children under the age of seventeen were deported from France, most to their deaths.[4] The French rescue agencies were able to save about seven thousand children, smuggling many to Spain and Switzerland.[5]

Resistance Groups Outside of France

France was not the only country where resistance groups were motivated by the desire to save children. In Belgium and the Netherlands, thousands of children were hidden in homes, monasteries, hospitals, and boarding schools. Hirsch Grunstein lived in an underground children's home in Belgium when he was sixteen:

> There was . . . an organization called la Comité de Defense des Juifs [Committee for the Defense of the Jews]. It was an underground organization with the sole purpose of helping out, of having a network of people that rescued Jewish children. They had scouts scouting for would-be hosts. They had scouts that were scouting for children in need where others didn't know any more what to do—just about to be caught. . . . They had people that went about paying. . . . They had nurses and doctors going around to provide medical care. That was the Comité de Defense des Juifs. They had 2,500 Jewish children. It was an underground organization in touch with the Belgium underground. It was founded by a Jewish professor in Brussels.[6]

As quickly as the national resistance movements hid Jewish children, the Nazis tried to find them. When they did, they shipped them to concentration camps and, after 1942, to the death camps. Jewish children in Belgium were transported to the holding camp at Mechelen and then to Auschwitz. Grunstein came close to being on one of those transports. His home was one of the ones to be evacuated:

> The Germans had the intention of collecting us, and [Adolf] Eichmann sent his deputy Anton Mueller—called the "Bloodhound of Vienna." He did such a good job [of finding Jews in hiding] in Greece, in Salonika, in

Hirsch Grunstein walks down De Keyserlei Street in Antwerp, Belgium, on his way to school on June 30, 1942. Grunstein lived in an underground children's home in Belgium when he was sixteen.

Vienna. He came to collect us. A telegram
was sent to the German commandant of the
concentration camp Mechelen where the Jews
were shipping out—to be prepared for to
receive all these children and to ship
them out.[7]

But before the children could be gathered up, a half-Jewish
worker at Mechelen discovered the plan:

That commandant had a secretary by the name
of Lise Lotte. Her father was in the German
Wehrmacht [army]; her mother was Jewish.
They lived in Antwerp. The story as I
heard it—it may not be totally accurate—
[was that] they were taken to Mechelen.
The mother made a big fuss, [saying,]
"My husband is a soldier in the Wehrmacht
fighting for Germany and you do that to
me?" Apparently the bargain was [reached]:
You go back to Antwerp. Your daughter, who
speaks perfect German, French, and Flemish,
stays with me as my secretary.[8]

With the help of two other Jewish camp inmates, the secretary
got word of the upcoming raid to the underground:

In that camp there was a Jew who was the
beer-man for the Germans. . . . His task
was to provide beer for the Germans in the
camp. He had contact with a beer distribu-
tor. The beer-boy was the liaison with the
underground. The house Jews had contact with
the underground. A house Jew became the
lover of Lise Lotte. Lise Lotte was the first
one to read the telegram from Adolf Eichman.
She didn't hand it right away to the

commandant. Apparently she waited twenty-four hours and told [the house Jew] first. He told the beer-boy. The beer boy told the underground. Six homes out of the seven homes were dispersed that night [the people left]. Convents, schools . . . institutions, private people. One home with all its children spent the night in the woods.[9]

Sabotage

While some resistance movements in Western Europe focused on rescue, others concentrated on disrupting the German army. The groups often started loosely. In France, young men went into hiding to escape from being forced to do work for the Nazis.

A member of a French Jewish resistance group, Arnold Einhorn, poses outside wearing a rucksack the night before he escaped across the border into Spain.

Eventually, these men came together in groups called Maquis, named for the high ground where they hid. Groups such as the Maquis were not Jewish, but Jews in France, Belgium, Denmark, and the Netherlands, joined these movements as their only means of resisting the Nazis.

Bertha Goldwasser was such a woman. A Jew born in Poland, she had moved to France. She was arrested with other Jews and was on her way to a concentration camp. She pried boards loose from the floor of the train car and jumped through the open space. A non-Jewish family found her, set her broken leg, and cared for her. When she recovered, she became part of one of the Maquis:

> Until liberation I joined the French resistance and worked with them until the liberation of Paris. . . . The French resistance worked very hard, and did . . . a lot for the Jews. . . . When they heard that Jews were being arrested they "sent" immediately and took the Jews into the forests. They were organized in a military manner, and we worked against the Germans. . . . We were after the [German] military. When a [German] military unit would pass, [the resistance] threw grenades, and they hampered in general . . . their advance.[10]

Sabotaging German army operations was only part of the military work of the resistance. Members also helped the soldiers fighting against Germany. Goldwasser assisted in that work, too:

> We also had aviators, American, Canadian, and English, who had been shot down, fell [parachuted] down. The planes were shot down. These people, the American aviators,

when they were sick or wounded, we picked
them up and brought them to the Spanish
as well as to the Swiss border. I myself
led twenty-four Canadian aviators to the
Spanish border. And there I handed them
over to other members of the resistance
and also to clergymen. They dressed them in
different clothes and led them to Spain.[11]

Erika Goldfarb was a member of the French Armée Juive
(Jewish Army) when she was a teenager. Her job was to get materials to the right people:

I went down and joined Jewish Army . . .
and swore allegiance. It was all very hush-
hush. . . . I was Alice Renault in the
Secret Army. [What kind of training were
you given?] Not much. I was given a little
bit of money and told, "Buy yourself a
handbag . . . big enough to put stuff in.
I was a courier. I did Nice, Toulouse,
Lyon—a triangle. I was transporting things.
. . . I transported stuff from one place
to another with suitcase. But I never,
never asked what was in them. . . . Later,
I knew. They were radio transmitters for
the Maquis in Southwestern France, and
they needed all that stuff. And they needed
arms, too, of course. I escorted people who
were supposed to go to Spain.[12]

Forging Identities

The underground resistance also forged identity papers. These
false documents enabled Jewish people to pass as Gentiles. Young

A collage of forged French identification papers and rubber stamps used to make them. Forged identity papers were a necessary tool in resistance movements and helped many Jews escape Nazi capture.

people, often young women, aroused the least suspicion in this operation. Yvette Frydman was one of those young women. She received very simple instructions:

> [My contact] said, "I will give you a port-
> folio, a briefcase with some things inside.
> You will pick it up at a certain address
> three times a week. You will take the
> Underground [Paris Metro]. You will get off
> [at] a certain station and go to another
> address and give it to a certain person.
> This is all you have to do—three times a
> week."[13]

As easy as it sounded, Frydman still worried. She was not very concerned about the danger to herself, but to the operation:

> Right away I told her, "I'm very willing
> to do this, but I don't want to go to a
> special address to pick it up and I don't
> want to go to a special address to deliver
> it because if I am caught and the Germans
> give me two slaps on my face, I will give
> both the addresses because I am not the
> very courageous, heroic type. . . . If they
> beat me, I'll say everything I know. It
> seems to me that somebody should give me
> the briefcase somewhere on the street and
> I should take it on the Underground and I
> should give it to somebody I don't know.
> . . . But if I know, I will talk."
>   So she said, "Well, you are really very
> honest."
>   I said, "Yes, I know myself."
>   She said, "OK. I'll have somebody
> give you the briefcase at a certain place

> three times a week. You take it in the
> Underground and you give it to another
> person when you get out of the
> Underground."[14]

Frydman followed the plan, and successfully completed her job numerous times:

> I got three identity cards: one for myself,
> two for my parents. I could use mine
> because I speak French. Of course, they put
> another place of birth. They never change
> the date of birth because they said that
> under pressure a person cannot remember
> a new date of birth. So I had to memorize
> everything. And I got two identity cards
> for my parents which were only to be used
> in case of life and death . . . because as
> soon as they opened their mouths you could
> see they were not born in France.[15]

The resistance movements in Western Europe rescued thousands of children, sabotaged hundreds of German factories and installations, and mounted armed attacks against Nazi interests. Although they were not led by Jews, many Jews filled their ranks. These movements gave the Jews of Western Europe a way to fight against their enemy. This was not the case in the East.

Chapter Four

QUIET RESISTANCE

On September 1, 1939, Hitler's war against the Jews began in Eastern Europe. He had driven a large portion of the Jews of Germany and Austria into Poland. On September 1, his army invaded Poland. It continued eastward until it entered the Soviet Union in July 1941. In less than two years, more than eight million Jews had come under Hitler's regime.

Hitler's plan was to turn all of Eastern Europe into *lebensraum*, or living space, for "Aryan" Germans. There would be no place for Jews. But he could not rid his territory of so many people right away. He had to wait until he was powerful enough so that no one could oppose him. In the meantime, he would herd the Jewish people together into ghettos, very small sections of cities, so they would be easy to deal with when the time came. And he would beat them down mercilessly.

Life in a Ghetto

So in the conquered lands of the east, Hitler's Nazi overlords issued one heartless decree after another. Chaim Kaplan, who kept a diary of life in the Warsaw ghetto in Poland, described the people's reaction to one of the unjust laws. The law was issued soon after Germany took over Poland, before the people were forced into ghettos:

> The forced labor decree gnaws away at
> our people. Because of the extent of the
> catastrophe, the Jews do not believe that
> it will come to pass. Even though they know
> the nature of the conqueror very, very well,
> and his tyrannical attitude toward them has
> already been felt on their backs; even though
> they know he has no pity or human feeling
> in relation to the Jews—in spite of all
> this, their attitude toward the terrible
> decree he has published is one of frivolity
> [because they believe it will not last long].[1]

But the catastrophe *did* come to pass. And it grew uglier. More decrees corralled the Jews into ghettos. Conditions in the crowded ghettos were deplorable. Food was rationed, and it was never enough. Diseases raced through the cramped quarters. Heavy restrictions and cruel punishments were imposed. Still, the people did not resist. On February 16, 1940, Kaplan wrote:

> There is no room in our inner feelings
> for despair and depression. We greet every
> edict with a deprecating [wishing evil
> away] smile, although we are conscious that
> the creators and enactors of these cruel
> decrees are psychopaths. . . . A poison
> of diseased hatred permeates the blood of
> the Nazis, and therefore all their stupid
> decrees, the fruit of this hatred, are
> doomed to failure. Such an awareness saves
> us from despair. Anything founded upon
> insanity must not last long.[2]

But the insane cruelty lasted longer than five more years. Its suddenness made resistance nearly impossible. A thirteen-year-old

Conditions in the Warsaw ghetto were horrible. Food was scarce and people died daily from disease and starvation. Jewish vendors sell vegetables in a market in the summer of 1941 (top). Below, a body lies on the street in Warsaw.

boy described in his diary the beginning of the ghetto of Vilna, Lithuania:

> The streets are closed off. . . . The streets are turbulent. . . . A ghetto is being created for Vilna Jews.
>
> People are packing. . . . The women go back and forth. They wring their hands. . . . I go around with bleary eyes among the bundles, see how we are being uprooted overnight from our home. Soon we have our first view of the move to the ghetto . . . a gray black mass of people goes harnessed to large bundles. . . .
>
> People fall, bundles scatter. . . . [They] drive us on, do not let us rest. I think of nothing: not what I am losing, not what I have just lost, not what is in store for me. I do not see the streets before me, the people passing by. I only feel that I am terribly weary, I feel that . . . a hurt is burning inside me. . . . I feel that . . . my freedom is being robbed from me, my home, and the familiar Vilna streets I love so much. I have been cut off from all that is dear and precious to me. . . .
>
> The little streets are still full of a restless mass of people. It is hard to push your way through. I feel as if I were in a box. There is no air to breathe. Wherever you go you encounter a gate that hems you in.[3]

Even if the Jews had the time to resist, they did not have the means. Everything had been stripped from them. Their Gentile neighbors dared not help them. In fact, many of them were nearly as antisemitic as the Nazis. A teenager from Warsaw felt the hate of his Polish neighbors:

> They had the chance to show how the anti-Semitism was built in . . . in the people of Poland. It was so built in, the anti-Semitism for those people that they . . . even if they lost the country, they still have won their anti-Semitism against the Jewish people. . . . I was in a camp [in Poland]. . . . I could have run away from that camp. I could have just walked over the fence. Where am I gonna go? Who I am gonna go [to]? I was working with Polish people. . . . Next to me there was a Pole. He saw that every day I looked skinnier. I didn't have a glass of water. I didn't have bread. Nothing! . . . They had all those holiday breads. . . . It hurts you so much that you were living in a country for so many years . . . and the people turned their back on you, actually turned their back on you.[4]

Frank Bleichman was nineteen when the Jews in his town of Kamionka, Poland, were ordered into the Lubartów ghetto. Because he looked "Aryan," he evaded the roundup and took refuge among Polish farmers. He described his treatment among the non-Jewish Poles:

> They were hunting us, the German, Polish police and the Polish collaborators. . . . Jewish women, when they went to villages to buy food, they were intercepted from the Polish hoodlums, collaborators; some were

```
killed. They were robbed, beaten, and
called all kind of dirty, anti-Semitic
names.⁵
```

Resistance was difficult because it was punished severely. A survivor of the ghettos, the work camps, and the death camps gave this reason that so many people submitted to the abuse "like sheep, without lifting a finger in their defense. It is very difficult to raise a finger against a machine gun. It was also difficult to live knowing that because of my foolish act ten men have been executed, and there are widows and orphans."[6]

Smuggling

In the ghettos, resistance focused on survival. Smuggling food into the ghetto was the only way to remain alive. Usually, children had the best chance of smuggling successfully. Charlene Schiff, twelve when Hitler took over her city, described how she found food for herself, her mother, and her sister outside the ghetto of Horochow:

```
Ingeniously, we dug out two holes in the
fences, below the fences, so that a child
could sneak out to the other side and, you
know, take off the Star of David and try
to act like a normal human being and see
if we could obtain food. And now and then,
children brought home some food back to the
ghetto. I did it many times. It was very
dangerous, because if one was caught one
would pay with life. I mean, this was the
order, to shoot, to kill the person, the
perpetrator. I was very lucky, and now and
then I would bring a slice of bread, I
```

would bring a carrot, or a potato, or an egg, and these were very, very great achievements. My mother made me promise that I wouldn't do it anymore, but I disobeyed.[7]

Not every foray into the Aryan side succeeded. And every attempt carried the risk of death. Schiff came close to dying for her bravery:

There was one time when I snuck out of the ghetto and I was lucky to obtain two eggs, and I remember I was wearing a dress with little puffed sleeves, and I put an egg in each sleeve and tried to make my way back into the ghetto. I paid for these two eggs with a small gold ring that had a ruby in it that my mother sewed into my coat. I was quite proud of myself, and I just could picture my mother's and my sister's faces when they came home and we had two eggs to eat. Just before I was entering the hole, the camouflaged hole back into the ghetto, a Ukrainian guard spotted me, and he ran over and he started screaming at me, and he found the two eggs and threw them on the sidewalk and made me kneel down and rubbed my face in them, and screamed at me to get right back where I belong and never to show my face again on the outside. I was petrified, and I didn't give away the hiding place, the hiding entrance. I marched back into the ghetto, or he threw me back into the ghetto and that was the end of that. . . . He could have killed me.[8]

A young boy caught smuggling by a German guard in the Warsaw ghetto. Many young people tried to smuggle food into the ghetto to help their families survive.

Food was not the only item smuggled into the ghettos. Information was critical to people who were cut off from the rest of the world. If they knew when an *Aktion*—a raid—was going to take place, they could hide. If they heard from relatives, they might be encouraged. Getting information out was also important. The Jews wanted the world to know what happened to them. Some "Aryan-looking" Jews acted as couriers, carrying news in and out of the ghettos.

Again, young people—teenagers—were best suited for this work. They were not tied down with the responsibilities of family. Leah Hammerstein was eighteen when she became a courier between the Krakow ghetto and the Plaszow camp. Maintaining her "Aryan" identity gave her more than a few scares:

> I was sitting in front of a big basket with vegetables, cleaning it, and the sun rays came on my head and one of the girls said, "Look, her hair is reddish like a Jewess." And everybody laughed, and I laughed most hilariously, you know. But inside, you know, the fear was gnawing on my insides, you know. At another time the kitchen chef grabbed me and put my head on the table. He was preparing the, uh, the sausage for the evening supper. And he put this long knife to my neck and said, "You see, if you were Jewish, I would cut off your head." Big laughter in the room, and I laughed most hilariously, of course. But you know what it does to a psyche of a young girl in her formative years? Can you imagine? With nobody to console you, with nobody to tell you it's okay, it'll be better, hold on. Total isolation, total

loneliness. It's a terrible feeling. . . .
There is nobody you can go to ask for help.
You can nobody ask for advice. You had
to make life-threatening decisions all by
yourself, in a very short time, and you
never knew whether your decision will be
beneficial to you or detrimental to your
existence. It was like playing Russian
roulette with your life. And it was not
only one incident. It was this way from
the moment I came on the Aryan side.[9]

Early Deportations

From April 1940, when the first ghetto was sealed off, until
December 1941, when the first death camp opened, deportations
occurred. A deportation was a transfer of people from the ghetto
to another place, usually a camp. The deported people were all
loaded onto trains—cattle cars—with only a few possessions for
their journey. At first, no one knew where they were going. The
Nazis said they were being "resettled." Vladka Meed, seventeen
when she went into the Warsaw ghetto, was puzzled when the
trains arrived:

We didn't want to be deported. We under-
stood the deportation mean devastation in
the best way or concentration camp or even
killing, but how to prevent it we didn't
know at that time. We didn't understand
that it really means absolutely evacuation
of the whole ghetto. . . . We wanted to
believe that not the whole ghetto will be
deported, and it took quite a long time
till the truth about that everybody will be

deported went into the minds of the ghetto
people. And the young people realized it
faster than the others. The young who were
organized and who start to get the news
from other couriers [about] what is taking
place . . . in other parts.[10]

When the ghetto residents realized the awful truth, they began
to resist. Secret organizations sprang up in the ghetto workshops.
The largest was called the ZOB for its Polish name, Zydowska
Organizacja Bojowa, which means Jewish Fighting Organization.
Meed joined the group in the Warsaw ghetto:

We already organized also ourselves . . .
in . . . illegal groups. . . . We knew that
more or less information we had from the
underground, that people are being taken to
camps and . . . some people will be killed
and some people will be gassed. . . . At
that time we in the shop decided, the illegal youth group, that if they will come to
take us, we will stand up. We will not let
[ourselves] be taken away.[11]

Meed wanted to do more than wait for the Nazis to take her.
She wanted to fight back. Her fair skin permitted her to do just
that; at the age of twenty she became a courier for the underground
resistance group:

I didn't have any part in anything and I
was in a little bit depressed . . . not to
get anything to do. . . . Then the leader
. . . came over to me and told me that you
have a Polish document and you look Polish
and you will go out on the Aryan side,

Vladka Meed began working for the Jewish underground in the Warsaw ghetto.

on the Polish side, on the outside of the ghetto, the other side of the ghetto. And I was really at that moment elevated. I felt that after all something important is going to happen to me, and my features are work- ing for me. So they gave me a mission, and they told me that in a few weeks, somebody will look, come to your place and give all other information. This was the most, the high point of my remaining in the ghetto after the family was taken. It was not a question of being afraid. It was just the

opposite. It was the feeling of being
something which means I can do something,
a challenge which I was eager to take. And
this was how the underground really singled
me out on the other side to be the courier.
I didn't pick it for myself. I was only
proud and happy to be chosen.[12]

Meed listed some of the activities of the organized resistance:

Their aim was to start looking for places
to hide as many children as we are able to,
and to start buying and looking for arms

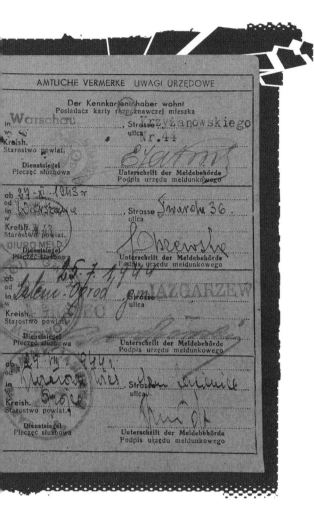

Vladka Meed used this false identification card while working as a courier for the Jewish resistance group in the Warsaw ghetto.

and to supply them, to smuggle them into the ghetto. I met . . . other young people. They are preparing the so-called Molotov Cocktail bottles [small bombs], and I saw couriers. . . . They gave me sometimes jewelry to smuggle on the other side and to sell it and buy for them dynamite or other things.[13]

Finding, purchasing, and smuggling weapons and dynamite into the ghetto took great courage. Young women were often entrusted with this important task. They could move about the Aryan side more easily than Jewish men. Most Polish men were serving in the army, so any young man seen in the Gentile sector aroused suspicion. Although she was excited to work in the resistance, Meed was also frightened:

It was not easy, especially for people like me. I didn't have any idea how a revolver looked or how dynamite looked, or even to get in contact with Polish people was not easy. You have to remember . . . not to look at the Pole and they should not find you as a Jew. . . . I remember the first revolver I bought from a smuggler, and I brought it to . . . somebody to check it. I didn't have any idea how it's supposed to work, if it's good or if it's bad. It turned out to be OK. I paid a large amount of money. I got it through illegal contacts and ways. . . .

I made the contact with the ghetto through telephone, certain calls, that I will be at this and this particular place and they have to wait for me and I will smuggle this into the ghetto.[14]

Meed had more than one close call:

[From the Aryan side] I came there [to the wall of the ghetto] with my package [of dynamite] in greasy paper that it should look like butter. And I paid the foreman. . . . When I came on top, going on the ladder on top of the wall, suddenly shooting was heard from far away, and they got scared. They snatched the ladder away and I was sitting on top, not being able to go back into hiding. They ran away. All of them hide. And I was with my package on top of the wall. And the shooting got closer and I was sure that I, at this time, I am done. I didn't see anybody on the Jewish side and I didn't see anybody on

the other side, and I [was] on top.
I didn't know what to do. I was afraid
to jump. I was afraid that maybe dynamite
can blow up. I didn't know even if it
can. I didn't know too much about dynamite.
But suddenly from the Jewish side, two of
my colleagues from the Jewish underground
saw me, came running to the wall. They made
a human ladder and they brought me down,
and we run away while shooting came very,
very close.[15]

The weapons and dynamite that Meed and others carried into the Warsaw ghetto were so little against the armed might of Nazi Germany. But they were enough to take down a few of the enemy. They were enough to allow some to escape. They permitted at least some resistance.

Chapter Five

FIGHTING BACK IN THE GHETTOS

The aim of the resistance in the ghettos was to keep the Jews from being deported to the camps. The Nazis had set up a massive system of camps. The first ones were concentration camps, built to hold prisoners. As more of Germany's men and materials were spent on war, the Nazis needed laborers to produce weapons and supplies. They turned the concentration camps into work camps and built hundreds more. But the Jews of the ghettos were not being transported to the labor camps. They were being sent to their deaths.

On December 8, 1941, the Nazis opened their first annihilation camp in Chelmno, Poland. The purpose of the death camps was to kill all the Jews imprisoned in the ghettos. Hundreds of thousands had already been slaughtered. They had been murdered by firing squads, sadistic guards, brutal labor, starvation, and exposure to the elements. But the main purpose of the death camps was to kill as many Jews as they could as quickly as possible. Four death camps were built and two concentration camps were converted into death camps. All six were located in Poland, near the ghettos. They were the means by which the ghettos were to be liquidated, or emptied of their Jews.

When the truth about the camps finally reached the ghettos, it was too late for most. But in at least sixty places, the residents, mainly the young people, mounted a resistance. The first was the ghetto of Lachwa, on September 2–3, 1942.

Resistance in Lachwa

Florence (Feigele) Gittelman, almost fourteen, worked outside the ghetto, digging ditches. Her father and brother were part of the underground, so she had heard talk of a revolt. But when it came, it was sudden:

> I came [home] in the middle of the night from my work. This ghetto was already surrounded by trucks, ammunition, guns. There were soldiers all around the ghetto. German soldiers. There were already Polish people,

A group of Jews being forced into cattle cars during a deportation from the Warsaw ghetto. Armed resistance began to occur more often once Jews learned about the deportations to the death camps.

peasants; they were already standing there looking into the ghetto. But mostly trucks . . . with all kinds of ammunition on the trucks. When we came in, I knew right away. I mean, you didn't have to ask questions. So nobody said a word to each other. We had two ghettos and there's a street separating us. . . . I was in the second ghetto. The young people, they were accumulating themselves, mostly men, in the first ghetto in case they're going to start taking us on trucks to kill. They gonna to try to break the gates and see how much, how many people could be saved. Run. Saved. You can't save your child, you just run. Whatever will happen will happen. So we knew.

I came into the [first] ghetto. Nobody was sleeping anymore. My mother was waiting for me. My father and brother wasn't there anymore. I asked them where they are, and my mother said to me, "They are in the other ghetto getting organized. Maybe they'll be able to run." And everybody was already crying and yelling. . . .

I hide under the covers. . . . All of a sudden, my mother said to me, "Feigele, come out of there."

I said, "What's the matter, Ma? Are we gonna get killed?"

He [sic] says, "We gonna get killed, but not you. . . . Don't ask questions. Here, put this on." She put in one of her red little rubies she had from her ring . . . and she said, "You go to the second ghetto. I don't know what's going to happen. You might get killed there, too," she said, "but people are going to try and run from there. They're going to rip the gate. This is what they made up, so you go there."

. . . I ran. I saw other people standing there. I tried to open the gate [to the second ghetto]. The gate was closed already, locked. You couldn't go through anymore. I started . . . banging, and they wouldn't let me through. They said, "Too late."

All of a sudden, I see—I hear shooting. I see fire. I see the buildings are burning. The other ghetto, not this ghetto where I lived. So I guess the

> "I got up and I ran. I ran over people, not over the ground, over people."

Germans thought *well, she gonna die anyway. Why—let her in, this kid, you know*. So they opened the gate [between the two ghettos], and they did let me—I was the last one to cross the gate from one ghetto to the other.[1]

The men of the resistance knew Lachwa was being liquidated. They planned to set the first ghetto on fire and break down the gate to the outside under the cover of flames and smoke. Armed only with sticks and stones, they would push their way through the lines of soldiers waiting to take them away. Everyone who could run would flee to the swamps and forests. Florence was still in the second ghetto when the uprising began:

It was really chaos. Everything was burning. Everything was shooting on everybody. I didn't know if the gate was ripped or not. . . . Every building was on fire, and people were just falling right in front of me. Just like flies, shooting, blood all over the place.

All of a sudden people are running in this direction towards the gate [to the outside]. And I'm running, and they are running and I am running. And people are just falling in front of me. I step over. I don't know if they were alive or dead, or just falling full of blood. I didn't look. I was running. All of a sudden, something hit me, and I fell. I fell on two people, and there were people on both sides of me. I see blood all over me. I touched myself. I said, "I'm alive. Get up. I'm alive. Run." I got up and I ran. I ran over people, not over the ground, over people. . . .

We ran to the main [square]. . . . And we came to a place by the name of Pripet. It was [a river]. And the Germans were still chasing us, I guess. When I looked back, and I saw the whole town was on fire already. . . . [My girlfriend] saw me, she says to me, "Feigele," she said, "look at you. You're all ripped to pieces." My whole back was ripped. My shoulder was ripped. She said, "Well, whatever will be will be." If I'll live, I live. If I'll die, I'll die.[2]

That was the sentiment of the resisters in all the ghettos: I may live or I may die, but I will fight. The biggest uprising took place in the Warsaw ghetto. The largest of the ghettos, Warsaw had the largest organized resistance movement. The ZOB, the Jewish

Mordecai Anielewicz was the leader of the ZOB, the Jewish Fighting Organization in Warsaw. In this group portrait taken in 1938, Anielewicz is at right in the back row.

Fighting Organization, was made up mostly of young people. The youngest was only thirteen. It was led by twenty-three-year-old Mordecai Anielewicz.

Uprising in Warsaw

By January 1943, the unspeakable became obvious to the Jews of Warsaw: The Nazis planned to murder everyone in the ghetto. Three hundred thousand Jews from the city had already been "resettled." Anielewicz urged the people to refuse to get on the deportation trains and to fight back. Vladka Meed, a courier who snuck in and out of the ghetto, helped spread the word:

> There were bulletins published by the Fighters Organization and they were put up on the walls of the buildings in the ghetto, and people are reading it. And the bulletins were calling for resistance, to build bunkers and not to let themselves be taken out, taken away, because the ways are leading to concentration camps. It's not resettlement to other working places, and are leading also to destruction, to death, and they should remember it. Don't let yourself be taken away.[3]

The fighters of Anielewicz's organization heeded his call. When the troops came on January 18 to begin the ghetto liquidation, most of the Jews went into hiding. Only about one thousand people reported for the deportation. Among them were a number of young Jews of the resistance. At a signal, they fired their few weapons at the Germans. The soldiers were caught completely off guard. The Polish underground newspaper *Dzien* (*The Day*) reported:

> The street was in the hands of the Jewish fighters for fifteen to twenty minutes. Only large reinforcements of the police enabled the Germans to gain control of the situation. The armed resistance made an extraordinarily strong impression on the whole ghetto; it was received with great enthusiasm by the whole Jewish community. The old Jews blessed the fighters. The bodies of the dead were kissed on the street.[4]

For about four days, the German soldiers and police tried to round up Jews for extermination. They were able to deport only sixty-five hundred people. When the standoff ended, ten

> "The old Jews blessed the fighters. The bodies of the dead were kissed on the street."

Nazi soldiers and hundreds of Jewish fighters were dead. But the resistance had scored a victory. The fighters had succeeded in stopping the deportations, even if only briefly. They had stood up to the enemy and the enemy had backed down. They had injected hope and pride into a discouraged people. Meed felt optimistic:

> You had the feeling that the ghetto is going to be led not by the country but by the people who are in the underground. They were listening to them. And this took place after January 18 in the Warsaw ghetto when it was the first organized small resistance and the Germans stopped the deportations. So from that time on, the atmosphere in the

> ghetto changed and I would say that
> the uprising and the role of the Jewish
> Fighters Organization in the Warsaw ghetto
> . . . succeeded . . . because they had
> the cooperation of the remnants of the
> population, of the Jewish population in the
> ghetto. They work like together. They were
> listening to them.[5]

The people were listening not to the Jewish elders, but to Anielewicz and his young fighters. Their limited success inspired others to resist. Meed explained:

> That January 18 and the deportation which
> stopped after the little resistance of the
> organized Jewish group, it gave the people
> the thought and also the belief that, after
> all, you can resist, and the German will
> be afraid. They stopped deportation because
> of the Jewish resistance. . . . After all,
> they can control a little bit their own
> destiny. So hiding appealed to them.[6]

The people hid underground. More than six hundred bunkers lay beneath the buildings of the ghetto like a giant honeycomb. Under Anielewicz's direction, the people stocked them with what food and weapons they could get. The stunned Germans had left the ghetto alone while they gathered more forces.

The Final Stand

The soldiers and police returned on April 19, 1943. It was the eve of the Jewish holiday of Passover, the day before Hitler's birthday. The Germans planned to liquidate the ghetto as a birthday present for their leader. They expected the action to only take three days.

Jews fought bravely during the Warsaw ghetto uprising. Nazi soldiers razed buildings to drive the Jews out into the streets.

Rachel Nurman, a young seventeen-year-old fighter, described what happened:

> Our leaders came through the roofs. . . .
> There were others fighting, but it was
> impossible to fight against such an empire.
> But . . . on April 19 . . . our fighters
> threw [the Germans] back. All of a sudden
> . . . the people start running and the gre-
> nades were thrown. They said, "This is the
> Jewish fighters!" And the Germans run and
> there was a lot of casualties in the German
> people. A lot of Germans fell dead.[7]

The Nazis, taken by surprise at the fierceness of the attack, retreated. The resistance proved to be stronger than in the January revolt. About 750 young men and women were part of the organized fighting force. They were no match, however, for the thousands of soldiers the Nazis could send in against them. The Nazis came into the ghetto again. Anna Heilman, fifteen at the time, described the scene:

> Hell broke loose. My sister was across the street and I was in this little post. There were maybe four of us. There was one rifle. . . . There were sniper shots all over. We didn't have radios. Our communicators were runners, young boys mostly, who were running from post to post to keep contact. One of the runners was running and [my superior] Shimmon saw him down the street. He was shot and he was wounded. So Shimmon run to bring him back and he was killed right then and there. Another runner came through and said, "Listen, guys, everything is over. Each one for himself, finished." . . . We got orders not to be caught alive, that no matter what happens, we are not going to go on the trains alive. Those were the orders. This was the spirit of the uprising.[8]

The spirit of the uprising was fierce and determined. But the Nazis were also determined. Heilman remembered what happened on the third day:

> The Germans were methodically blowing up and putting fires to every single building in the ghetto. . . . Our apartment was so hot, it was so smoky that we couldn't possibly stay there. . . . In the courtyard [the Germans] were with the rifle, with

The Nazis finally suppressed the Jewish fighters in Warsaw on May 16, 1943. After twenty-seven days of fighting, the ghetto was mostly destroyed.

their rifles, screaming, "Raus! Raus!
Raus!" [Out! Out! Out!] and shooting. And
the smoke was so dense that you couldn't
see. And people were jumping from all the
windows right into the ground. There was
no other way out. But because of the smoke,
they couldn't see. My sister, the runner,
and I jumped from the third floor down into
the asphalt-covered courtyard. We scraped
our knees and elbows, nothing else. We kept
on running, right through them. This runner
knew the bunkers ways, the other ways,
the little passages. And we were running
through the burning ruins of the ghetto,
through the part where the buildings used
to stand but weren't standing anymore,
into the sewers. And we can smell the gas
chasing us.[9]

The Nazis had released poisonous gas into the bunkers and the
sewers. From her post in a kitchen, Rachel Nurman watched
the Germans flush out all the pockets of resistance:

[The Germans] discovered the bunkers
which the Jewish people was hiding in them.
[There] were a lot of bunkers and they
came and they put gas in the bunkers and
the people died. Mordechai Anielewicz, our
biggest leader, died in that bunker. . . .
They shot immediately whenever they saw
leaders. They shot them at point blank.[10]

The outnumbered resistance fought for twenty-seven days,
until May 16. At least seven thousand Jews died in the fighting.

More than fifty thousand were captured. Most were sent to the death camps. Heilman was captured on May 5:

> We were surrounded by the Germans and taken to *Umschlagplatz* [the main square] and then we walked through the ruins. There wasn't one building left erect. The smell is indescribable. It is the smell of rubber, noxious. . . . And the ruins of the ghetto made it in mountain-like sights, and you could see on the top, people, single people, like rats, putting their head up, disappearing, looking at us, darting from one burning hole to another, like specters. . . . And then came the time that we were marched out to the cattle trains.[11]

"The smoke was so dense that you couldn't see. And people were jumping from all the windows right into the ground."

The Warsaw ghetto uprising ended in death for nearly all the ghetto residents. But some did survive. Some escaped through the sewers to the Aryan side. Some, like Vladka Meed, were on the Aryan side when the revolt began. The survivors took the account of the brave resistance to other ghettos and camps. The story of the Warsaw uprising encouraged Jews in other places to rise up against their oppressors even though they were greatly outnumbered. In Białystok, for example, a few hundred young fighters armed with one machine gun, a small number of pistols, Molotov cocktails, and bottles filled with acid held off the Germans long enough for a few dozen prisoners to escape. Many other ghettos formed resistance movements, including Vilna, Kraków, Grodno, Mir, and Minsk. These resistance movements succeeded only in helping some escape to the forests outside the ghettos.

Even such small successes were important. They kept hope alive. They fueled the will to resist. Those who escaped continued to fight.

Chapter Six

RESISTANCE TO THE END

Between 1933 and his death in 1945, Hitler established about twenty thousand camps in the land he controlled. Some were very large; others were small and temporary. They served different purposes. Concentration camps housed people who had been arrested for anything the Nazis considered crimes. Prisoner of war (POW) camps were for soldiers captured in war. Labor camps had factories where inmates made items for the Germans. Transit camps held people until room could be made for them at other camps. Six annihilation camps were used primarily for murder: Chelmno, Belzec, Sobibór, Treblinka, Majdanek, and Auschwitz.

As in the ghettos, Jews in the camps generally did not resist the cruelties of their captors. Organized resistance came only after 1943, when the Jews realized the choice was to fight or die. By that time, the population of the camps was largely adolescents and young adults. People under fourteen and over sixty were usually the first to be killed. Many of the older inmates died from the harsh conditions and brutal treatment. The heartiest lived the longest, and they were often the ones in their teens and twenties.

Small Acts of Sabotage

Before any resistance was organized, some people found ways to defy their Nazi guards. Leopold Page, in his late twenties, was supposed to produce rockets for the German war effort in the Bruennlitz labor camp. He made sure the rockets would not fire:

> I was a welder. What I did? I have to weld certain parts of the machinery, so I opened . . . the bottle with the gas overnight, very little. In the morning was no gas. So I could report that we don't have gas, I cannot do the job. So they got me another bottle. Couple of days happened to the other bottle. So we couldn't finish it. I said, "It's not my fault that they're putting wrong gauges on the machine. I don't do anything. I try to work, and then I cannot do it." Well, we were doing some little job, but this was a little type sabotage.[1]

Selma Wijnberg Engel was almost twenty-one when she was deported to the death camp at Sobibór. She was taken to the work section of the camp. She knew her job was temporary; everyone who worked at Sobibór would eventually be killed. Still, she looked for little ways to hurt the Nazis:

> We had to sort the clothes . . . from first quality, second quality, and I know everything went to Germany. And I try, every piece what I saw, I tried to tear it apart, the clothes, and I thought that was the only thing what I could do of sabotage. And also when I found money and jewelry, I didn't give it to the Germans. . . . I didn't even think that we ever can use it for ourself. I was just thinking, only thinking whatever I thought, how can we do, on the sabotage against the Germans.[2]

Selma Wijnberg Engel (at center, standing) was deported to the Sobibór camp. She tore apart clothing being sent to Germany as a way to resist the Nazis.

Even though the acts of sabotage were small, saboteurs risked not only death, but torture. To prevent such resistance, the camp guards often punished many for the offense of one person. Alan Zimm, who was twenty-three in 1943, witnessed Nazi retaliation for sabotage at the Dora-Mittelbau camp:

> Somebody sabotaged a part in the factory
> there. Not in our group. In another group.
> They destroyed a part of the, of a machine.
> Without the machine they couldn't finish the
> . . . rocket. So they, without the part the
> rocket was unfinished. There was no way they
> could finish it. What they did, they took
> two hundred people from that compartment,

from that group. And, uh, put gallows in
the middle of the factory, in the tunnel,
and hanged every one of them. They hanged
them in pairs, the two. And everybody working in that factory, had to go into the
tunnel, line up, and walk through under-
neath the gallows where the, the, those
200 people were hanging and come back
to our work. They say, "See what's going to
happen if you do the same thing what they
did? You will hang."[3]

Despite the risk, sporadic acts of sabotage continued. Thomas Blatt, sixteen when he arrived in Sobibór, observed: "They killed us for every little thing—you don't go straight; you don't sing—because we were ordered to sing when we are marching."[4] They could be killed for standing silent as well as for sabotage. The Nazis killed prisoners for no reason at all.

Blatt gave an example of how small, and yet how satisfying, some of the sabotage could be. Because he was young, he had been chosen to be camp guard Frenzel's shoeshine boy. Blatt took every opportunity to oppose the enemy:

One day, Frenzel called me . . . gave me
a rake and told me to go and clean up the
hallway, this corridor, because the next
500 people were coming [for extermination].
I was raking the sand and something was
going between the teeth of the rake. When
I bent down, a little piece of paper. I
picked up some paper, and I looked close
and it was money. . . .
We talk about the resistance—we associate
the resistance with guns. What is this? [It

A postcard from Sobibór dated June 18, 1942, written by Alice Elbert. Some Jews in the camp found small ways to resist the Nazis.

is] a spiritual resistance. Imagine: going to dead [die] and still sabotaging . . . taking the time and ripping the paper into little pieces so it would be of no use to the Germans. This is really heroism![5]

Organized Resistance

Organized resistance in the camps followed much the same pattern as in the ghettos. Many did not realize the desperate nature of their plight until 1943, when the death camps were in full swing. Even then, people debated the wisdom of outright defiance, as Blatt recalled: "I remember the talk of resistance. The young people were saying, 'Let's fight back. We'll die anyway.' And on the other side were voices from family men like my father: 'It's no use. We'll die anyway. Let's die as a family.'"[6]

In several of the camps, the young people won. They united with the common goal of surviving and escaping. They hid children, covered for those who were sick, and organized sabotage operations. At three camps—Treblinka, Sobibór, and Auschwitz—they revolted. They had no illusions that they could overthrow the camp rulers. Blatt described their reasoning:

We knew our fate. We knew that we were in an extermination camp and death was our destiny. We knew that even a sudden end to the war might spare the inmates of the "normal" concentration camps, but never us. Only desperate actions could shorten our suffering and maybe afford us a chance of escape. And the will to resist had grown and ripened. We had no dreams of liberation; we hoped merely to destroy the camp and to die from bullets rather than from gas. We would not make it easy for the Germans.[7]

Revolt at Treblinka

That attitude of desperate defiance drove the resistance at Treblinka to plot an attack. About one hundred men devised a way to get weapons. Their plan was to overpower the camp guards with everyone acting at the same moment. Then they would set fire to the camp, climb the fence, and escape. They hoped that at least some would reach the safety of the forest that bordered the camp. Twenty-one-year-old Kalman Teigman noted that the youngest in the camp were vital to the plot:

> Two children of the Hofjuden [children with special privileges] were employed in polishing the shoes of the Germans, and they worked in the hut where there was an arms store. This store was built by the experts amongst the Hofjuden, the fitters and the construction workers. An extra key to the store had to be made. And, in fact they made a key, and the children were to go into the store, to remove arms in sacks, and to place them on refuse carts—guns, bullets, hand grenades and revolvers.[8]

The first part of the plan worked as intended. The children got the weapons to the men. The second part, Teigman explained, was carried out by the men: "We were to ask the SS men to come to all the workshops and these places, under various pretexts, and to kill them inside the workshops, and in this way to rid ourselves of most of the SS men. And this is how, it turned out in fact."[9]

However, the sudden surprise attack on the guards in the watchtowers did not take place after the mistaken rifle shot confused the conspirators. Massive chaos ensued. Teigman described his escape:

> I simply climbed over the fence. There had already been people who had escaped that way, and on the fence there were already blankets and boards, and we climbed over on these. . . . The Germans chased us on horses and also in cars. Some of those who escaped had arms. I also ran with a group that possessed a rifle and revolvers. These people returned the Germans' fire and the Germans withdrew. In this way we managed to reach the forest which was near this camp.[10]

Sobibór Uprising

The most successful revolt was at Sobibór. Located in a dense forest deep in Poland, Sobibór was built to keep people in—the ones who would not be murdered immediately. Samuel Lerer, a twenty-one-year-old member of the resistance, described the elaborate system for preventing escape:

> There was a mine field and barbed wire [around the camp]. There was a man-made water [moat] and there was machine gun towers all around and there was a tank in there. There was about 300 or more Ukrainians [guards] all with machine guns

and guns. And beside that there were about 60 high-ranking German SS.[11]

In its seventeen months of existence, a number had tried to resist. Every attempt was brutally crushed. Leon Feldhendler thought these attempts failed because too many people were involved. He organized a resistance movement in the camp but purposely limited it to thirty or forty carefully chosen people. One was sixteen-year-old Thomas Blatt, who knew why he was selected:

> I was a young kid; I shouldn't be involved in the organization direct but I was involved for two reasons. Because I was the boss . . . of the place where they burned the papers and this was a place where a German could easy be called in and killed and nobody will see it. And Leon Feldhandler . . . lived in Yestiva and was a friend of my dad's. He know me very well. . . . There was a few of us young people who was able to move about more easier than the grown-up people.[12]

Philip Bialowitz, at fourteen, was one of the youngest who knew Feldhendler's plan. Like the others, he was motivated by the certainty of his own death:

> We knew our end is going to end in the extermination camp. But our aim was that one person should get out of Sobibór and to tell the world what happened here. The chances for survival in Sobibór were null. So we started to organize—about forty people started to organize, making a revolt.

> In the forty people, there was only about
> ten or twelve who were in close circle.
> They were like the main command. My brother
> was in this group to which they make a
> revolt. We had six hundred Jews and we were
> afraid for the Jews themselves so there
> shouldn't be any informer. . . . We made
> the meeting in secret.[13]

But thirty or forty "city Jews" were not enough against three hundred armed guards. They needed someone with combat skill. They found that person on September 23, 1943. The Nazis were liquidating the Minsk ghetto, sending the last residents to Sobibór. In that transport was prisoner of war Sasha Pechersky, a lieutenant in the Russian army. Together, Feldhendler and Pechersky devised a plan. Blatt described what the prisoners would do:

> The plan was very simple. It was divided in
> two phases. The first phase . . . was the
> killing of the Nazis, killing them quietly,
> without arousing any suspicion with knives
> and axes. The second phase was that after
> killing when we assemble for the roll call.
> We should . . . have an open revolt and use
> the guns we'd get when we killed the
> Germans.[14]

Phase 1 was to be carried out by the resistance group; no one else knew about this operation. Blatt expected it to be relatively smooth:

> When we planned the revolt we took into
> consideration the very well-known disci-
> pline of the Nazi SS officers. . . .
> [The camp had] little shops—a tailor shop,

This is a group portrait of participants who survived the Sobibór uprising on October 14, 1943. This picture was taken in August 1944. Leon Feldhendler is in the back row at the far right.

a shoemaker shop—which were for the Nazis.
. . . So we planned that the tailor shop
. . . should make an appointment with the
head [guard] for [a particular] time. The
shoemaker's shop for another time. . . .
They were very well assured they will come
at the time. If a German will tell you he
will come at that time, you can be sure
ninety percent he will come.[15]

After the guards were killed, Blatt explained, the leaders would invite the inmates to join in the second phase:

We should escape in an orderly manner. It
was planned we should assemble in our normal

```
groups and march to the main gate because
Sobibór had . . . little cages . . . and
gates lead from one cage to another one. So
we will march out like it's a German order
because the guard will think it's a German
order. And we will come closer to the gate
where the machine gun is . . . and the
guards will see that something's not OK,
but it will be too late and we will over-
whelm them.¹⁶
```

The teenagers had mixed feelings as they anticipated the action. Blatt was eager: "I was impatient. I was scared . . . not really to die because I had time to get used to it. I was scared I would suffer. We prisoners . . . always said, "We will not go to the gas chamber." We wanted to be shotted [*sic*]."¹⁷

Philip Bialowitz hoped for the best, but he was prepared for the worst:

```
One day before the uprising my brother [who
worked in the pharmacy] came over to me and
he told me like this. "Take a couple jars
of jewelry and hide it under the trees,
about two or three feet down. In case we
survive, we'll have something that . . .
will help us. And he brought me a bottle of
cyanide [poison] and a compass. If you get
injured, I should drink the bottle because
they'll burn the people alive. And if you
survive, the compass should show you how
to get out from the woods because [it] was
about 25 to 30 radius forest.¹⁸
```

When the day came, Phase 1 went off nearly as planned. In an hour and a half, the resistance killed eleven SS (Nazi special security force) officers and a number of Ukrainian guards. Bialowitz served as a messenger:

> I had to relay to the main command that the Gestapo is dead already. Whenever they killed somebody, I ran into the command. Pechersky was there; I gave him the report. We killed one by one to the shoemaker, to the watchmaker. They came to the appointment to meet death. We killed ten Gestapo and one Ukrainian.[19]

The second phase did not go as smoothly as they had planned. A Ukrainian guard spotted the body of one of the dead Germans. The guards began to shoot and the prisoners ran toward the barbed wire fence. Half of the six hundred people in the camp made it out. However, all but about fifty

"They came to the appointment to meet death. We killed ten Gestapo and one Ukrainian."

were killed by the mines or by Nazi patrols that hunted them down. Very soon afterward, the Germans killed the half who did not escape and shut the camp down.[20]

Uprising at Auschwitz

Resistance at bigger camps was more difficult. Auschwitz, the largest of all the camps, was a huge complex of three main camps and about forty subcamps. Auschwitz II, also called Birkenau, was the death camp. In all but Birkenau, most prisoners did what they were told, hoping simply to survive until the war's end. But

Members of a Sonderkommando 1005 unit pose next to a bone crushing machine in the Janowska concentration camp. Jews in the Sonderkommando in Auschwitz were forced to work in the crematoria to help hide the atrocities the Nazis committed.

resistance formed in Birkenau. The only prisoners who stayed alive there were the *Sonderkommando*. They worked in the gas chambers and the crematoria—the ovens that burned the bodies of those who were killed. In 1944, they knew that they, too, would be killed. They decided to revolt.

At the same time, in another part of the camp, a few young girls were also thinking of a rebellion. Anna Heilmann had witnessed the Warsaw ghetto uprising. She had been a courier for the resistance in the ghetto. She survived because she remained on the Aryan side when the uprising started. Now, in Auschwitz and only sixteen, the spirit of defiance still stirred in her:

> It began this way. A small group of
> girls were getting together after work
> in Auschwitz dreaming of Israel, singing
> Hebrew songs and talking about life outside,
> or in the future, if we survive. . . . We,
> too, decided that we were not going to let
> ourselves be taken without a struggle. . . .
> We were about seven or eight girls, no
> more. Out of this friendship evolved the
> ideas of resistance. . . . What could we
> do, each one of us, to resist?[21]

They were actually in a unique position to do something. Some of them worked in an armaments factory. That factory manufactured the parts and supplies for the weapons of the German army. The girls worked with explosives. Heilmann described what happened:

> The gunpowder was within our reach. We
> thought, "We can use it!" Somebody in the
> group knew that the Sonderkommando was pre-
> paring resistance. We said, "Let us give
> the gunpowder to them!" We gave it through
> Marta to Anitchka who was working in
> Birkenau. She ran between Auschwitz and
> Birkenau and gave it to Roza Robota. Roza
> Robota gave it to the men in the
> Sonderkommando.[22]

The men in Birkenau used the gunpowder to make crude grenades. The men killed three guards and set fire to one of the camp's four crematoria and a gas chamber. But the damage was not enough for any to escape. The Nazis quickly and brutally put down the revolt. They uncovered four women's roles in the plot and hanged them publicly.

The greatest success of the resistance in the camps was not the damage they caused or the Germans they killed. The greatest success was that they permitted many to escape. The escapees generally took refuge in the forests. From there, they continued to resist the Nazis.

Chapter Seven

PARTISAN GROUPS IN THE FOREST

The strongest civilian resistance against the Nazis took place in the forests of Eastern Europe. To hide the camps, the Germans had built them deep in the woods of Poland. The ghettos also were often close to forests. So the people fleeing Hitler and the Nazis made their way to the forests.

Escaped Jews were not the only ones in the forests. Polish and Soviet people, both soldiers and civilians, had also fled German brutality. They formed groups known as partisans. Partisans were makeshift soldiers. They organized themselves like army units and fought guerrilla warfare. That is, they made small, quick, sneak attacks on their enemy.

Living in the Forest

Frank Bleichman, sixteen when Germany invaded his native Poland, became a guerrilla. When the Jews in his city were to be relocated to the Lubartow ghetto, he went instead into the forest. At first he found only a few other people in hiding there:

```
My group was twelve. Other groups were
thirty, forty. . . . My first group must
have . . . got killed around the beginning
of '43. . . . We had no experience, how to
operate, how to behave, how to secure our-
selves by traveling and things like that.
```

> All happened by mistakes which we learned
> later on.[1]

Bleichman made many mistakes, but he managed to stay alive. Eventually he found other people who were also running from the Germans. His little group grew and cooperated with others:

> We joined with other . . . group, and there
> were about over fifty, something like that.
> And then we joined with the Gruber's Group,
> which, they were POWs from Lublin who had
> escaped. And in general we later grouped
> together—not one group, just we worked
> together because it was impossible to make
> a huge group in our area to stay together.
> We were in contact. We performed all kinds
> of missions together, uh, plans and things
> like that, and we were separate. We're not,
> we're not too far away—like fifteen, twenty
> miles away from each other. And we got
> stronger every day.[2]

Some of the partisan groups were made up of only Poles, some were only Russian, and some were only Jewish. A few were mixed. Bleichman found that some of the partisans would not accept Jews into their ranks: "The Jews who would find themselves Polish partisans, they were many times abused or . . . they didn't feel comfortable. The ones who . . . didn't look like Jews, they were hiding their identity. The others in the Russian partisans, they were not discriminated."[3]

The Jews in the forests often stuck together in all-Jewish groups. But some of the other partisans did not like the idea of independent Jewish bands. The Jews had to prove themselves.

This photo of a Polish communist partisan unit was taken in the Parczew Forest, near Lublin, Poland, in 1944. Some of these units allowed Jews while others did not.

Bleichman learned how to be tough: "[In] some areas . . . they didn't let, uh, Jewish partisans to be independent. They tried right away to disperse them. . . . So we tried hard and we showed them that we can do our job. When they gave us missions, we fulfilled, and we remained [independent]."[4]

Bleichman's unit, although "under the umbrella [protection] of Polish partisans,"[5] remained fiercely independent:

```
We did not want to be together . . .
because we had our obligations, and we
felt what we're going to do, we're going to
get credit for. And otherwise we would be
sweeping floor or shining shoes with them.
We showed them that we could fight as good
```

103

or sometimes as better than they are. And the reason was that we had nowhere to go. Our direction was to fight. Or to kill or be killed. They had homes intact, they had families, they had somewhere to go back to. We did not have that. So . . . we could not even surrender. You see, the beginning what we thought why they trusting us, they were trusting us, the people's army, people, you know, the . . . Polish partisans, better than their own because they knew that we cannot surrender, because surrender meant dead by torture. We had nowhere to go, just that one direction: fight. Fight. Everybody who was in our path, our enemy, we didn't care; we had to defend ourselves. And that's the way we remained.[6]

Obtaining Weapons

The first order of business for partisans was to obtain guns. Bleichman's group started with nothing: "The only firearms at that time we had is make believe. We organized ourselves [with] pitchforks. We broke off all the teeth, one tooth left on, and put a strap on the handle, and over shoulder—from far away it looked like a rifle."[7]

When they did acquire guns, the quality was not the best. Bleichman's first weapon was "a small caliber pistol with no bullets. The handle was falling apart. . . . We had a rubber band to put it on. It was an old one."[8]

But without real guns, they could not defend themselves or fight the Germans who came into the forest looking for Jews. Bleichman used the fake weapon to obtain real ones. He heard of a farmer who had a hidden stash of rifles. He went with a few men, make-believe guns, and the broken pistol with no bullets:

> I didn't know . . . what I'm going to tell
> him. . . . I had no choice. I couldn't say
> no. I was, uh, speaking very fluent Polish.
> I also had a mustache, and I wore a, uh,
> policeman, Polish policeman's overcoat,
> and I had also a badge on my lapel. I
> don't know where I got it from—was in a
> ski hat. . . .
>
> I found the house. . . . A man opened
> the door. . . . [I told him], "We heard
> that you have firearms, and would like you
> should give us of your free will. If you
> don't we have to use force." I don't know
> where I got this, uh, speech from, but
> somehow this came to my mind.[9]

Bleichman got six weapons that night. Another Jew in hiding, Harold Zissman, who was twenty-one when he entered the forest outside the ghetto of Derechin, obtained firearms from a different source:

> I told [the head of the forest resistance]
> that I was sort of the leader of the group.
> . . . He says, "Tell me, what you're doing
> is good. But what do you think—we have
> warehouses here with weapons? I know you
> want to join. We'll take you in. Where are
> we going to get weapons for you?"
>
> I says, "Where do you get weapons for
> the others? Tell me and I'll get them."
>
> "Well, you've got to go kill a policeman
> or German."
>
> I says, "We are ready. Whenever you go

105

```
to, that you are going to do these kinds of
ways, to set up an ambush, we volunteer."
     . . . We were going to have an ambush.
     . . . I was elected to climb up on the
tree and be the observer. . . . So we went
on that ambush and succeeded. And I ran to
get, the first thing I got was a pistol and
I got a gun from somebody else, I mean a
rifle from somebody else. And before long
. . . all of us had weapons. . . . I felt
myself right now ten feet tall. Here I got
a pistol, got a rifle. . . . I was full of
joy, full of hope that now I'm doing some-
thing worthwhile.¹⁰
```

Once they had weapons, the partisans had to figure out how to use them. Most of the escaped Jews had no military experience. Bleichman observed: "A gun was worth more than a million dollars, because . . . at least you could defend yourself with something. . . . It took us about two weeks; we learned very quickly how to operate, how to fight, you know, and everything else."¹¹

The Jewish partisans put the weapons to good use:

```
We got into fights with the German gendarmes
[police], and . . . we began already start
making sabotage acts. Uh, we went, uh, to
disarm a group of . . . about two dozen
Germans. . . . We had a shootout with them
for several hours, and we had to pull away
because we could not get reinforcements
they could get. . . . We did not sit hiding,
but we look for action. And then we had a
lot of fights.¹²
```

Members of the Bielski partisan group in the Naliboki Forest in Belorussia.

Always on the Move

In the forests, the Jewish groups had to fight the Nazis who raided the forests periodically looking for Jews. Sometimes they had to defend themselves from antisemitic Poles. Bleichman recalled being constantly on the move: "We organized ourselves, sophisticated system where we could live. First of all, we kept tight security. Every day we were stationed in another place. Twenty kilometers this way, twenty kilometers south, north. Never stayed longer than one day in one place."[13]

If the lives of fighters on the run were difficult, imagine the plight of families. In Belorussia, entire families fled the ghettos into the vast, jungle-like Naliboki Forest. A number of Jewish groups welcomed men and women, young and old. They set up family camps with kitchens, workshops, and schools. One of the largest, founded by three brothers, was the Bielski Group. Fela Abramowicz described life in the Bielski family camp:

> We washed in the forest waters whatever was available. And we slept in our clothes. We didn't undress. We went to the toilet in the bushes; there was no paper, so had to use leaves. We had food. The men all had guns. . . . [We] made big fires in forest and went to gather food at night and slept around the fire. One side would get very hot; the other side would get frozen. Then all of a sudden we [would be] attack[ed].[14]

This group portrait of former Bielski partisans was taken in the Foehrenwald displaced persons camp, April 3, 1948. More than 1,200 hundred Jews survived in the Bielski partisan group.

Liberation

The attacks finally ended in the summer of 1944. The Soviet army liberated Belorussia and the partisans came out of the forests. More than twelve hundred had survived in the Bielski Group alone. In all the family camps, about ten thousand lived.

Almost a year later, in May 1945, Germany surrendered. Of Europe's nine million Jews, three million survived the Holocaust. Some survived by their wits, some by luck, and some through the bravery of others. A good number survived because of the determination and the courage of resistance fighters.

The spirit of those fighters was expressed in a poem written by Hirsch Glick, who was nineteen when his town of Vilna became a ghetto. When the Nazis liquidated the ghetto and he was sent to a camp, he and eight others resisted by attempting to escape. All nine were killed. But Glick's poem, translated into seven languages, was sung in camps and forests wherever Jews resisted Nazi cruelty. It became known as the "Song of the Partisans":

> Never say that there is only death for you
> Though leaden skies may be concealing days of blue—
> Because the hour we have hungered for is near;
> Beneath our tread the earth shall tremble: We are here!
>
> From land of palm-tree to the far-off land of snow
> We shall be coming with our torment and our woe,
> And everywhere our blood has sunk into the earth
> Shall our bravery, our vigor blossom forth!
>
> We'll have the morning sun to set our day aglow,
> And all our yesterdays shall vanish with the foe,
> And if the time is long before the sun appears,
> Then let this song go like a signal through the years.

This song was written with our blood and not with lead;
It's not a song that birds sing overhead,
It was a people, among toppling barricades,
That sang this song of ours with pistols and grenades.

So never say that there is only death for you.
Leaden skies may be concealing days of blue—
Yet the hour we have hungered for is near;
Beneath our tread the earth shall tremble: We are here![15]

TIMELINE

1933

January 30—Adolf Hitler becomes chancellor of Germany.

1935

September 15—First of the Nuremberg Laws is published, taking rights away from Jews.

1938

October 28—Deportation order returns seventeen thousand Germans of Polish ancestry to Poland.

November 9–10—Kristallnacht (Crystal Night) or Night of Broken Glass; Nazi-instigated rampage against Jews.

1939

September 1—German invasion of Poland begins World War II.

October 26—Forced Labor Decree requires Polish Jews age fourteen to sixty to work for Germans.

1940

April 30—Ghetto in Lodz, Poland, is sealed, imprisoning 230,000 Jews.

May 10—Germany invades France, Belgium, Holland, and Luxembourg, and hundreds of thousands of additional Jewish people come under Nazi control.

1941

June 22—Germany invades Soviet Union, which has a Jewish population of three million.

December 8—First of six death camps is opened at Chelmno, Poland.

1942

January 20—At conference in Wannsee, Germany, Nazi leaders discuss "final solution," the extermination of Jews.

May 18—Baum Group bombs anti-Communist and antisemitic display at Berliner Lustgarten.

August 10—Two hundred armed Jews escape the Mir ghetto in Belarus without a fight, joining the partisans.

September 2—First ghetto uprising occurs in Lachwa; one thousand escape, of whom about 120 are able to join the partisans.

1943

January 18—First uprising in Warsaw ghetto halts deportations.

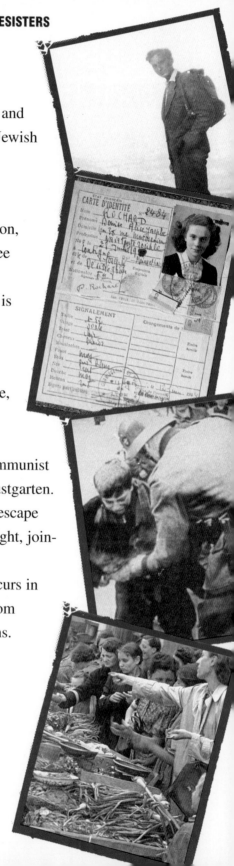

February 18—Hans and Sophie Scholl are caught distributing the sixth Leaflet of the White Rose. Four days later they, and other members, are executed.

April 19–May 16—Warsaw ghetto uprising ends in liquidation of the ghetto.

June 11—Nazis order liquidation of all remaining ghettos.

Summer—Armed resistance in Bedzin, Bialystok, Czestochowa, Lvov, and Tarnów ghettos.

August 2—Revolt at Treblinka death camp. Two hundred escape but are hunted down.

August 15–19—Bialystok ghetto underground revolts; all involved are killed; 1,200 children are deported to Theresienstadt camp and then to Auschwitz.

September 1—Vilna ghetto uprising. A few escape.

October 14—Revolt at Sobibór death camp. Three hundred escape, of which about fifty survive.

1944

July 24—Soviet army liberates Majdanek concentration camp and partisans come out of forests.

August 6—Last ghetto—in Lodz,
Poland—is liquidated.

October 7—Revolt at Auschwitz destroys
one crematorium and one gas chamber.

November 10—Barthel Schink of Edelweiss
Pirates is publicly hanged in Cologne,
Germany.

1945

January 27—Soviet army liberates
Auschwitz death camp.

May 8—Germany surrenders
unconditionally, ending World War II
and the Holocaust.

CHAPTER NOTES

Introduction

1. Samuel Willenberg, "I Survived Treblinka," in Alexander Donat, ed., *The Death Camp Treblinka* (New York: Holocaust Library, 1979), p. 208.
2. Ibid.
3. Ibid., pp. 208–209.
4. Ibid., pp. 210–211.
5. Ibid., p. 212.
6. Gerald Reitlinger, *The Final Solution: The Attempt to Exterminate the Jews of Europe, 1939–1945*, 2nd Revised and Augmented Ed. (New York: Thomas Yoseloff, 1961), p. 153.

Chapter 1. Living With Persecution

1. Joseph K. Fortunoff Video Archive for Holocaust Testimonies, Yale University, p. 49, HVT-61. Cited in *Witness: Voices from the Holocaust*, ed. Joshua M. Greene and Shiva Kumar (New York: The Free Press, 2000), p. 23.
2. Mary Antin, *The Promised Land* (New York: Penguin Books, 1997), pp. 7–8.
3. Ibid., p. 9.
4. Henry Landman, *Survivor Testimonies*, United States Holocaust Memorial Museum (USHMM) Archives 1997.A.0175.
5. Ibid.
6. Carola Steinhardt, *Oral History Interview*, USHMM, RG-50.030*0368, pp. 3–4, June 3, 1996, <http://collections.ushmm.org/artifact/image/h00/00/h0000261.pdf> (January 14, 2009).
7. Lore Metzger, *Oral History Interview*, USHMM Archives RG 02.018.
8. Gad Back, *Oral History Interview*, USHMM, RG-50.030*0361.
9. Guy Stern, *Oral History Interview*, USHMM, RG-50.030*0223, pp. 2, 3, May 1, 1990, <http://collections.ushmm.org/artifact/image/h00/00/h0000193.pdf> (January 14, 2009).
10. Steinhardt, p. 5.
11. Ruth Drescher, transcript of address to Seton Hill University's Annual Kristallnacht Remembrance Interfaith Service, National Catholic Center

for Holocaust Education, November 8, 2005, <http://blogs.setonhill.edu/ncche/014329.php> (January 17, 2008).

12. Ibid.

13. Martin Gilbert, *Kristallnacht: Prelude to Destruction* (New York: HarperCollins, 2006), pp. 36, 118, 139.

14. Miriam Litke, letter to Martin Gilbert, June 12, 2005, cited by Gilbert in *Kristallnacht: Prelude to Destruction*, pp. 49–50.

15. Max Kopfstein, communicated to Martin Gilbert, June 6, 2005, cited by Gilbert in *Kristallnacht: Prelude to Destruction*, p. 43.

Chapter 2. Rebel Groups in Germany

1. Katie Kellerman, "The Edelweiss Pirates: A Story of Freedom, Love and Life," *International Raoul Wallenberg Foundation*, n.d., <http://www.raoulwallenberg.net/?en/saviors/others/edelweiss-pirates-story.3518.htm> (January 17, 2008).

2. Walter Meyer, *Oral History Interview*, USHMM, RG-50.030*0371, p. 21, August 2, 1996, <http://collections.ushmm.org/artifact/image/h00/00/h0000120.pdf> (January 14, 2009).

3. Ibid., pp. 25–26.

4. Ibid., pp. 21–22.

5. Kellerman, "The Edelweiss Pirates: A Story of Freedom, Love and Life."

6. Meyer, p. 27.

7. Ibid.

8. Ibid., pp. 27–28

9. Ibid., p. 28.

10. Ellen Arndt, *Interview by USC Shoah Foundation Institute for Visual History and Education, University of Southern California* (Rochester, N.Y.: April 14, 1997), interview code 28315, tape #2, time code 26:30.

11. Ibid.

12. Ibid.

13. Ibid.

14. "German Jews During the Holocaust: 1939–1945," *Holocaust Encyclopedia*, United States Holocaust Memorial Museum, <http://www1.ushmm.org/wlc/article.php?lang=en&ModuleId= 10005469> (February 24, 2008).

15. "The First Leaflet," The White Rose Society, n.d., <http://www.whiterosesociety.org/WRS_pamphets_first.html> (January 14, 2009).

16. "The Second Leaflet," The White Rose Society, n.d., <http://www.whiterosesociety.org/WRS_pamphets_second.html> (January 14, 2009).

17. Ibid.

18. Ibid.

Chapter 3. Resistance in Western Europe

1. Gaby Cohen, "Gaby Cohen," in Carol Rittner and Sondra Myers, eds., *The Courage to Care* (New York: New York University Press, 1986), pp. 66–67.

2. Ibid., p. 67.

3. Margot Blank, *Interview by USC Shoah Foundation Institute for Visual History and Education, University of Southern California* (Brooklyn, New York, 1998), interview code 39664, tape 4, segment 32, time code: 04:00.

4. Cohen, p. 68.

5. "Rescue of Children," Shoah Resource Center, n.d. <http://www1.yadvashem.org/odot_pdf/Microsoft%20Word%20-%205820.pdf> (November 11, 2008).

6. Hirsch Grunstein, *Interview by USC Shoah Foundation Institute for Visual History and Education, University of Southern California* (New York), interview code 41037, tape 7, segments 191–192, time code: 18:50, ID 41037-3.

7. Ibid.

8. Ibid.

9. Ibid.

10. Bertha Goldwasser, *Oral History Interview*, USHMM, RG-50.427*0019, August 4, 1946.

11. Ibid.

12. Erika Felicitas Goldfarb, *Interview by USC Shoah Foundation Institute for Visual History and Education, University of Southern California* (Toronto, Canada, 1995), interview code 4024, segment 11, time code: 10:20 and segment 12, time code: 15:30.

13. Yvette Frydman, *Interview by USC Shoah Foundation Institute for Visual History and Education, University of Southern California* (Tel Aviv, Israel, 1995), interview code 7098, tape 3, segment 61, time code: 02:12.

14. Ibid.

15. Ibid.

Chapter 4. Quiet Resistance

1. Chaim A. Kaplan, *The Scroll of Agony: The Warsaw Diary of Chaim A. Kaplan*, January 16, 1940, trans. Abraham I. Katsh (Bloomington: Indiana University Press, 1999), p. 103.

2. Ibid., February 16, 1940, p. 120.

3. Yitskhok Rudashevski, diary entry for September 6, 1941, in Alexandra Zapruder, ed., *Salvaged Pages: Young Writers' Diaries of the Holocaust* (New Haven, Conn.: Yale University Press, 2002), pp. 199–200.

4. Abraham Lewent, *Oral History Interview*, USHMM, RG-50.030*0130, Acc. 1989.H.0344, pp. 10–11, October 20, 1989, <http://collections.ushmm.org/artifact/image/h00/00/h0000004.pdf> (January 14, 2009).

5. Frank Bleichman, *Oral History Interview*, USHMM, RG-50.042*0006, Acc. 1994.A.447.

6. Joseph K., Fortunoff Video Archive for Holocaust Testimonies, Yale University, p. 49, HVT-61. Cited in *Witness: Voices from the Holocaust*, ed. Joshua M. Greene and Shiva Kumar (New York: The Free Press, 2000), p. 50.

7. Charlene Schiff, *1993 Interview*, USHMM, March 23, 1993, <http://collections.ushmm.org/artifact/image/h00/00/h0000178.pdf> (December 10, 2008).

8. Ibid.

9. Leah Hammerstein Silverstein, *1996 Interview*, USHMM, n.d., <http://www.ushmm.org/lcmedia/viewer/wlc/testimony.php?RefId=LSW0848F> (February 28, 2008).

10. Vladka Meed, *Oral History Interview*, USHMM, RG-50.030*0153.

11. Ibid.

12. Ibid.

13. Ibid.

14. Ibid.

15. Ibid.

Chapter 5. Fighting Back in the Ghettos

1. Florence Gittelman Eisen, *Oral History Interview*, USHMM, RG-50.030*0260, pp. 6–7, August 18, 1994, <http://collections.ushmm.org/artifact/image/h00/00/h0000209.pdf> (January 14, 2009).

2. Ibid., pp. 7–8.

3. Vladka Meed, *Oral History Interview*, USHMM, RG-50.030*0153.

4. "How the Warsaw Ghetto Is Defending Itself," *Dzien* (*The Day*), Polish underground newspaper, January 1943, cited in Wladyslaw Bartoszewski, *The Warsaw Ghetto: A Christian's Testimony* (Boston: Beacon Press, 1987), p. 68.

5. Meed, USHMM, RG-50.030*0153.

6. Ibid.

7. Rachel Nurman, *Interview by USC Shoah Foundation Institute for Visual History and Education, University of Southern California* (Tampa, Fla.: February 2, 1997), interview code 25692, tape 2, time code 22:30.

8. Anna Heilman, *Oral History Interview*, USHMM, RG-50.030*0258.

9. Ibid.

10. Nurman.

11. Heilman, USHMM, RG-50.030*0258.

Chapter 6. Resistance to the End

1. Leopold Page, *1992 Interview*, USHMM, n.d., <http://www.ushmm.org/lcmedia/viewer/wlc/testimony.php?RefId=LPB0563M> (February 28, 2008).

2. Selma Wijnberg Engel, *1990 Interview*, USHMM, n.d., <http://www.ushmm.org/lcmedia/viewer/wlc/testimony.php?RefId=SES0514F> (February 28, 2008).

3. Alan Zimm, *1991 Interview*, USHMM, n.d., <http://www.ushmm.org/lcmedia/viewer/wlc/testimony.php?RefId=AZD0044M> (February 28, 2008).

4. Thomas Blatt, *Interview by USC Shoah Foundation Institute for Visual History and Education, University of Southern California* (Brooklyn, New York, 1995), interview code 1873, tape 4, segments 26, 30, 31, time code 03:30.

5. Ibid.

6. Ibid.

7. Thomas Toivi Blatt, *From the Ashes of Sobibor: A Story of Survival* (Evanston, Ill.: Northwestern University Press, 1997), p. 139.

8. Kalman Teigman's testimony at the Adolf Eichmann trial, cited in "Treblinka Death Camp Revolt," Holocaust Education and Archive Research Team, 2009, <http://www.holocaustresearchproject.org/ar/treblinka/revolt.html> (November 12, 2008).

9. Ibid.

10. Ibid.

11. Samuel Lerer, *Interview by USC Shoah Foundation Institute for Visual History and Education, University of Southern California* (Brooklyn, New York, 1995), interview code 1609, tape 3, segments 25, 26, 27, time code 18:50.

12. Thomas Blatt, Interview.

13. Philip Bialowitz, *Interview by USC Shoah Foundation Institute for Visual History and Education, University of Southern California* (Little Neck, New York, 1997), interview code 32788, segment 17, time code 18:50 and segment 18, time code 15:00.

14. Thomas Blatt, Interview.

15. Ibid.

16. Ibid.

17. Ibid.

18. Bialowitz.

19. Ibid.

20. Richelle Budd Kaplan, "Escape Under Fire: The Sobibor Uprising," Yad Vashem On-line Magazine, 2004, <http://www1.yadvashem.org/about_yad/magazine/data6/Sobibor.html> (November 12, 2008).

21. Anna Heilmann, interviewed October 14, 1985, in *Women of Valor: Partisans and Resistance Fighters*, 2001, <http://www3.sympatico.ca/mighty1/valor/anna1.htm> and <http://www3.sympatico.ca/mighty1/valor/anna2.htm> (November 6, 2008).

22. Ibid.

Chapter 7. Partisan Groups in the Forest

1. Frank Bleichman, *Oral History Interview*, USHMM, RG-50.042*0006, Acc. 1994.A.447.

2. Ibid.

3. Ibid.

4. Ibid.

5. Ibid.

6. Ibid.

7. Ibid.

8. Ibid.

9. Ibid.

10. Harold Zissman, *Oral History Interview*, USHMM, RG-50.030*0318, n.d., <http://varian.ushmm.org/cgi-bin/Pwebrecon.cgi?v1=2&ti=1,2& Search%5FArg=Harold%20%20AND%20%20Zissman&Search%5FCode= CMD&SL=None&CNT=25&PID=5480&SEQ=20081209175802& SID=6> (January 14, 2009).

11. Bleichman.

12. Ibid.

13. Ibid.

14. Fela Abramowicz, *Interview by USC Shoah Foundation Institute for Visual History and Education, University of Southern California*, ID code 25114, tape 4, segment 113, time code 23:00.

15. Hirsch Glick, "Song of the Partisans," trans. Aaron Kramer, in Jacob Glatstein, Israel Knox, and Samuel Margoshes, eds., *Anthology of Holocaust Literature* (New York: Atheneum, 1982), p. 349.

GLOSSARY

Aktion—German word for "action." A raid in which Jews in ghettos were rounded up and sent to work camps or death camps.

antisemitism—Prejudice against Jewish people.

Aryan—Originally, people speaking certain languages. The Nazis used the term to denote what they called a race of people of Germanic background who were, typically, tall, blond, and blue-eyed.

"final solution"—The term for the Nazi plan to solve what they called the "Jewish problem" or "Jewish question" by killing all the Jews in Europe.

Gentile—A non-Jewish person.

Gestapo—*Geheime Staatspolizei*, literally "secret state police," the Nazi police.

guillotine—An instrument used for beheading people.

Gymnasium—The term in Germany for secondary school, or high school.

liquidate—The word used by the Nazis to mean the closing of a ghetto. Ghetto residents were shipped to annihilation camps and the ghetto buildings were destroyed.

partisans—Fighting units of people who organized themselves like army units.

propaganda—Speech, writing, or other form of communication aimed at persuading people to think or believe a certain way.

Schutzstaffel (SS)—Military-like organization. Members of the SS served as camp guards and police.

storm troopers—Men of the *Sturmabteilung* (SA), the Nazi private police force. Also called Brownshirts.

subversive—Attempting to undermine, or go against, authority.

Ukrainians—Prisoners of war from the Ukraine, an area in southwest Russia, used by the Nazis as guards in the labor and death camps.

FURTHER READING

Adler, David A. *Child of the Warsaw Ghetto*. New York: Holiday House, 1996.

Boas, Jacob, ed. *We Are Witnesses: The Diaries of Five Teenagers Who Died in the Holocaust*. New York: Henry Holt and Co., 1996.

Boraks-Nemetz, Lilian and Irene N. Watts, eds. *Tapestry of Hope: Holocaust Writing for Young People*. Plattsburg, N.Y.: Tundra Books of Northern New York, 2003.

Downing, David. *Fighting Back*. Milwaukee, Wis.: World Almanac Library, 2006.

Epstein, Helen. *Children of the Holocaust: Conversations with Sons and Daughters of Survivors*. New York: Penguin Group, Inc., 1998.

Gottfried, Ted. *Children of the Slaughter: Young People of the Holocaust*. Brookfield, Conn.: Twenty-First Century Books, 2001.

Holliday, Laurel, ed. *Children in the Holocaust and in World War II: Their Secret Diaries*. New York: Washington Square Press, 1996.

Kacer, Kathy. *The Underground Reporters*. Toronto: Second Story Press, 2004.

Stadtler, Bea. *The Holocaust: A History of Courage and Resistance*, rev. ed. New York: Behrman House, 1995.

INTERNET ADDRESSES

United States Holocaust Memorial Museum
   <http://www.ushmm.org/>

USC Shoah Foundation Institute
   <http://college.usc.edu/vhi/>

Yad Vashem, The Holocaust Martyrs' and Heroes'
   Remembrance Authority
   <http://www.yadvashem.org/>

INDEX

A

Abramowicz, Fela, 108
Anielewicz, Mordecai, 76, 78, 82
Antin, Mary, 11–13
anti-Nazi pamphlets, 32–38
antisemitism
    intensification of, 13–20
    in resistance groups, 102–103
    as routine, 11–13, 58
    violent expression of, 20–22,
        58–59
Armée Juive (Jewish Army), 49
Arndt, Ellen, 30–32
arrests, hiding people from, 22
athletics, discrimination in, 16–17
atrocities, condemnation of, 30–38
Auschwitz, 32, 44, 85, 90, 97–100

B

Beck, Gad, 16–17
Belgium, 43–46, 48
Belorussia, 107–109
Belzec, 85
Bialowitz, Philip, 93–94, 96–97
Bielski Group, 107–109
Birkenau (Auschwitz II), 97–100
Blank, Margot, 41–43
Blatt, Thomas, 88–91, 93–97
Bleichman, Frank, 58–59, 101–107

C

Chelmno, 70, 85
children, rescue of, 39–47
Cohen, Gaby, 39–41
concentration camps

avoidance of, 22, 63–64
    children in, 39, 44, 47–48
    deportation to, 20, 39, 44,
        47–48, 63–64, 76
    resistance from, 70, 85–100
courier activities, 49, 62–63,
    64–67, 76, 98
crematoria, 98–99

D

death (annihilation) camps. *See*
    also specific camps.
    deportation, resistance to, 76,
        83
    escapes from, 7–10
    as punishment, 32
    purpose of, 70
    resistance from, 70, 85–100
deportations, 20, 44, 47–48, 63–64,
    71, 76–84
disease, 55
Dora-Mittelbau camp, 87–88
Drescher, Ruth, 19–20

E

Edelweiss Pirates, 24–30
emotional effects, 62–63
Engel, Selma Wijnberg, 86–87

F

Feldhendler, Leon, 93, 94
food rationing, 55
forced labor, 33, 54–55, 70, 85–87,
    99
forest resistance groups, 101–109